NEVADA LIGHT BLUE HUMOR

11/3/99
Rick Gamble

By

Rick Gamble

Copyright © 1999 by Rick Gamble

ISBN 0-7414-0205-X

Published by:

Buy Books on the web.com
862 West Lancaster Avenue
Bryn Mawr, PA 19010-3222
Info@buybooksontheweb.com
www.buybooksontheweb.com
Toll-free (877) BUY BOOK

Printed in the United States of America
Printed on Recycled Paper
Published July-1999

To Charlotte, my wife of forty years, who has endured my obscure sense of humor, outrageous jokes and bad timing every one of those years!

ACKNOWLEDGMENTS

The problem with trying to thank all the people who have contributed in different ways to this work is that, invariably, major contributors, or people who think they were (but weren't) are left slap out. Yet, it is only meet, right and my bounden duty to make attribution to as many friends, relatives, neighbors, co-workers and others as possible, even though there may be some poor, sniveling schmoe sobbing in the shadows someplace. Alright! I'm sorry!! I'll catch you later in my next book, OK?

So, my thanks to the following people who have either given me ideas for one or several of these stories or were supportive (by laughing uncontrollably) when I practiced on them over the years. No, Harold, names aren't in alphanumeric or any other order. To find your name (if, in fact, it is even there) you're pretty much going to have to read the whole damned list. Clever, what?

Jim Pugh, Gay Roche, Dick and Judy Inskip, Ron Slaughter, Bob Hahn, Norma Beales, Judi Bailey, Ted Lokke, John P. Sande III, Craig and Mary Sande, John and Nikki Peterson, Bob Braman, Hilda Wunner, Billie Tout, Don Klassic, John and Sandy Mayes, Gary Lubra, Bob Beach, Ken Morgan, Cindy Osthus, Jim Buck, Dan Ryssman, Moe McGuire, John Busse, Bob Brown, Don Heath, Barbara and

Hall Goss, Rick Michaelson, Howie Tune, Dottie Bachelor, Debbie Bradly, Charlie Prebble, Wes Frensdorf, Gary Pryor, Paul Dieringer, Mark Gregg, John Scott, Gordy Nitz, Don and Christine Peterson, Bob Guin, Tom, Mary, Keeli, Taryn, and Tommy Killian, Les Moren, Tom Hood, Ken and Carol Allen, Doug Hackett, Susan Waters, Rob Bates, Debbie Myers, Ed Pierczynski, Norm and Jill Beesley, George Flint, Jim Schofield, Bud Beasley, Julie and Reyn Johnson, Debbie and Mike Fahner, Spiros Anastasatos, Laura and Waseem Akhtar, Dick Davies, Joe Midmore, Jim Joyce, Fred Hillerby, Diane, Richard, Mike, Laura and Meg Ganchan, Rich Dwyer, Dick Cavel, Ken Franklin, Wes and Ann Hall, John Williamson, Marvin, Patrick and Ryan Murphy, Bob Carroll, Eunice Hylin, Jeannie and Wayne Garrett, Bob and Helen Benson, John and Naomi Sande, Nelson Martin, Dave and Dar Galleron, Ron Newpauer, Rick Russell, Bob Stacy, Del Snyder, Jim and Carol Pitts, Bob McDonald, Rex Baggett, Billy and Margaret Pugh, Gene Small, Herman and Charlotte Hofer, John and Linda Pollard, Larry Seithel, Lowel Epstein, Al McCarty, Sara-Lee Fleischer, Cole Feinberg, Rusty Van Hoose, Mike Metzger, Rita Condos, Cat Bradley, Nancy Spinelli, Laura Kidd, George Charlton, Phil Gillette, Tom Williams and that sniveling schmoe sobbing over there in the shadows whose name I cannot recall right now!

TABLE OF CONTENTS

INTRODUCTION

Nevada humor is no different from humor elsewhere, I suppose...it's a wonderful state, one I have loved and called home for over a quarter century, but I have simply found some things are funnier here than in other states I have lived. The silver state is huge...over 110,000 miles, and most of it...some 87% is owned by the federal government. The Bureau of Land Management allows people to visit the land (most of it is unrestricted...except for the military areas, the bomb testing parts, and a strange place called 'Area 51') and periodically sells-off small portions for development. There is usually a clamor to buy it.

Nearly two million people call Nevada home and most of them used to call California home. Not that we Nevadans (I just have to be a native by now) have anything against Californians, but we wish they would please quit trying to make the 'Battle Born' state just like the state they left. Still they come and still they try to change us. Their success would spell doom for all of us!

I was in London once and talked briefly with a very proper, stodgy British woman who took offense too easily and with too much apparent pleasure. She asked where my home was in 'America' and on learning I was from western USA, commented she had heard things were rather primitive there. I had to agree with her that some things might appear that way and gave her a quick story about our western primitive.

"A man in Hawthorn, Nevada," I told her, "decided it was time in his life to rob a bank. He did so one morning with some dispatch, the law caught him with equal dispatch... before lunch! The traveling circuit judge happened to be in town at that time and the criminal was hauled into court, pled guilty, was sentenced. The police took him to the state penitentiary in Carson City that afternoon. The police drove over 100 miles per hour to get to the state lock-up because, on the open roads there were at that time no speed limits. On the way they passed several 'ranches'...euphemisms for houses of prostitution...which are legal in most of the state." I couldn't say much about our legalized gambling, because Brits have been legally wagering for many years, but I did say that Nevada was larger than England, Scotland and Ireland and that such distances in one state allowed for certain freedoms, one of which certainly had to be the freedom to be 'primitive' if one chose. Our lady Jones-Smyth threw up her nose, and as she turned to walk away muttered, "Bigga is naut necessarily bettah!"

Reno used to be the divorce capitol of the western world, maybe even the whole world. In just six weeks, one could become a resident of the state, un-hitch quite legally and get back home to start the whole process over again. Lots of women used to travel here, reside at a dude ranch or inexpensive motel for the required period, go through the motions at the court house on South Virginia Street, walk down to the nearest bridge and throw those hated wedding bands into the raging eleven inch deep Truckee River. A thriving business developed collecting those hated wedding bands out of that raging torrent. Some of the women stayed in Reno and lead useful and fulfilling lives, others got the hell out of Dodge as quickly as they could.

Conversely, chapels sprang up to provide equally quick weddings. Vastly more weddings are performed in the 'sagebrush state' than divorces. I met a guy one time in Carson City who called himself "Marrying Sam." He claimed to be the preacher All Capp depicted in his 'Lil Abner comics...remember him? "And with the five dollar weddin' I'll strip to the waist and rassle a live grizzly bar!"

Most Nevada towns have a wedding chapel or two and the variety of weddings is almost infinite...as are the prices. For under a hundred dollars a surprisingly nice wedding can be had.

As Nevada heritage is sparse, its history is even sparser. After you read about the early Mormon settlers, the Donner party, testing of nuclear bombs, Bugsy Siegel, organized crime and the rise of Casino gambling, mining, and after you read about Nevada's legalized prostitution you might just have read it all. But there is more. I'll try to tell you about Nevada humor.

Every story told in this work is true to the best of my knowledge (yeh, right!) All the stories originated here. Some may say that certain stories originated elsewhere, but do not believe it. These stories may have drifted elsewhere, good stories will do that. But herein lies the true accounting of the origin of some of the best, I think, stories in the land. If you don't mind revisiting some familiar stories placed in Nevada settings, then I'm certain you will enjoy my book.

I'm writing to entertain and bring back a few memories to those people who have good senses of humor, who enjoy the telling of a story.

A letter to friends from a couple who had moved from Columbia, S.C. to Reno in the summer of 1973.

March 29, 1974

Dear John and Linda,

Well, we made it all the way across the country in our new Ford station wagon, three daughters, one collie and doped-up cat. The vet gave us some tranquilizers to feed her along the way to keep her from going nuts in the car.

It's a totally barren land out here, folks! You have to go a long way to find a tree, even the sight of a Cottonwood is pretty exciting. We passed through the Great Salt Lake Desert on Interstate 80 that didn't have a bend or turn in it for almost 100 miles. In South Carolina, that would be almost the entire way from Columbia to Charleston.

When we came over the hill east of Reno and saw the Truckee Meadows, Charlotte almost cried. Not from the 'joy' of moving to her new home in the west, but from the starkness of the area so unlike her native South Carolina. It's a desolate place all right! The sun shines 85% of the time, the winds blow almost all the time and it rarely rains. The city gets all its water from the Truckee River and we all laugh when we hear it referred to as a 'River'... it is so small!

Steam comes out of the ground in several places south of town and we see wild horses every time we go up to Virginia City. Coyotes have the full run of the place. Charlotte plays the slot machines in the grocery stores and we go downtown to the smaller casinos and enjoy the cabaret shows. 'People watching' is one of our favorite diversions. Harold's Club has a swell gun collection. Back home there was a sign on the Savannah Highway that read "Harold's Club or bust!" It's just hard to believe we go there for entertainment.

The beautiful dutch colonial home we sold in Columbia would be unaffordable here in Reno...even if we could find one. We have settled in a nice ranch style home not nearly as big as the home we left. The girls were flashed by a pervert on the way back home from swimming lessons at Moana Pool and we called the police, but he had split.

The school system here seems to be quite good, they even provide school books to the kids at no costs...unlike Columbia schools. There is a junior ski program available to school kids so I guess my girls will grow up to be ski bums! There is no state income tax, the sales tax is the same as S.C. at 6%.

The first winter we were here it got down to ten below zero. We all feared we had made a serious mistake coming out here! The first summer we were invited to a swim party and could not go in the pool, it was so cold...it was June. The air is so dry it crackles! One plus is that cold drinks don't sweat, but we haven't gotten used to getting 'zapped' when one of us touches anything metal. That's a minus. Another plus, however, is that our animals don't have fleas or ticks...something about the altitude?

All in all it is a nice place. The people are all from someplace else and there is no stodginess anywhere to be seen. Remember how I complained about Charleston when we lived there? I used to say the Charlestonians were like Chinese. "They eat rice and worship their ancestors!" And that, simply being born in Charleston did not make you a native! The rule was that to be a true native, your people had to go back at least three generations. People here get a chuckle out of that! It is a young country and we feel we are going to enjoy it lot. But it does take a bit of getting used to.

For example, remember how we used to talk about the 'Red Light' district in Charleston and how as teenagers we would all pile in a car and drive slowly down 'West Street' to see if we could see some action? Well, in most of Nevada, prostitution is legal. In Reno (Washoe County) and Las Vegas (Clark County) there can be no 'legal' whore houses. It is a county option in the other 15 counties. There is a world famous brothel just 12 miles outside Reno... Did you ever hear of 'The Mustang Ranch?'

Sorry it took so long to write, but it has been quite a time for us. We hope you will come out for a visit. Tom Jones is performing up at Lake Tahoe and 'Rowan and Martin' and Paul Anka are due in the area soon. We have plenty of room and we would love to have you come see us...

Best Regards and Love, Keep in touch with yourselves!

Rick and Charlotte

THE COW COUNTIES

ALL IN FAVOR, RAISE YOUR ARMS

Several years ago, important people in Hawthorn, Nevada got together to come up with ideas for an event that would bring people from Reno and Las Vegas to town. Travelers were always happy to stop in Hawthorn...at the El Capitan... and pretty much just as happy to head out again. Hawthorn was famous in some circles as a major storage area for all the bullets and bombs left over from all the latest wars fought by our GIs. Except for the nearby Walker Lake, there was not much to draw people here.

The Hawthorn thinkers were accustomed to hearing people call their fair city "The Armpit of Nevada" and they didn't like that one bit. Yet, one wag said, "Why not? We could have an ARMPIT CONTEST, dinner, dance, flea market, ten kilometer jog, fishing derby, golf tournament...the works!"

"What kind of armpit contest?" quizzed one of the thinkers. "We could have two categories," said the originator, "we could have 'Hairiest armpit and smelliest armpit' and I bet 'Wide World of Sports' would cover it!"

This idea got a little press, but everyone asked to be a potential judge violently declined and the idea faded away.

❦

IT'S IN THE BOOK

Mary Ann McNish was the unofficial director of etiquette in Hawthorn for many years until her death in 1976. She was consulted on funerals, wakes and weddings, on teas, anniversary parties and, of course, on special occasions such as those rare visits by the governor at election time. On her last official consultation...a wedding between the mayor's daughter and the Ordinance Supervisor at the ammunition depot...she decided to make this her last, and best effort. She arranged for the couple to have counseling at the local Episcopal church. Then she had a sit-down to look over stationery selection, exact wording of the invitations, narrowing and expansion of the wedding lists, date setting, planning for the rehearsal party dinner, church programs, music and bird seed to throw at the newlyweds. She even had some ideas for their honeymoon! She was in her prime!

The big day came without a hitch. The crowd was, some thought, too big for the small church, but the music was outstanding, the minister was eloquent with his homily and the young couple were anxiously awaiting the final pronouncement that would be coming along any second now.

Something strange happened just before the rector proclaimed them husband and wife. A little man no bigger than 4 foot 9 inches ran among the pews pinching all the lovely ladies on their breast. When that was done, he resumed his seat near the back of the congregation and had no further part in the ceremony. The wedding ended after a little puzzlement, but all in all it was a swell occasion.

At the gala reception held at the El Capitan Casino, the wedding crowd was getting pretty liquored up. The mother of the bride approached Mrs. McNish proclaiming, "MaryAnn,

4

I want to thank you for all your help on the wedding, it was wonderful...everything was wonderful. I do have one question, however. What was that little man doing running all over the church pinching the ladies on their breast?"

"I went exactly by the book," replied Mrs. McNish as she opened the *Book of Etiquette* she clutched in her hand. "It says right here on page 88...'and just before the minister pronounces them married, a nervous little titter usually runs through the crowd.'"

❦

NAME THAT TOWN

How that town in southwest Arizona got named as told to me by Billy Johnson.

Over drinks and craps at the Mizpah Hotel in downtown Tonopah years ago, I was told a story by a man named Billy Johnson that sounded like it might be true. We were taking turns spinning yarns and throwing dice at the state's only ten cent craps table. "Bet big, win big," said Billy as he put a dime on the pass line and the "field." With vigor he tossed the dice and collected his winnings. He then put fifty cents on the "hard eight," threw the dice and won again. "The hard eight ain't the best odds, but when you win, you win big!" he exclaimed as he tossed the table a buck and came back to where I was sitting.

"Rick, it was the early days of this dusty little cross roads town with no name in southwest Arizona. You really couldn't call it a town, it was more like a collection of buildings that broke up the desert a little. There was a bar, of course, there is always a bar! Also nearby was a livery stable where a blacksmith could be heard in the cool of the morning banging on something or other and there was a mercantile store. The bar served whiskey, beer, some sarsaparilla, a root beer like drink. There was a table or two where you could eat a meal, that is, if the cook was sober. Out back was a building that had some bunks for the occasional overnighter who would wander through. That building was built uncomfortably close to the single seat outhouse.

"The only signs of life around the place was a tall, slim hombre they called Jim Leslie who fancied himself as a gunfighter. Jim had no experience in the gun fighting trade, however, he could draw and bust a bottle at about twenty-five feet—fast, too!

"That day Jim was doing his usual thing to pass away the time. He would stand on the porch in a menacing way, draw, twirl his handsome forty five's, and shove them back in their holsters. All day long he would do this.

"Jim Leslie barely noticed the small plume of dust coming down from the distant hills. Soon as he did, however, the tempo of his drawing, twirling, and shoving increased. Sometimes he would omit the twirling which was not his best activity.

"It wasn't long, maybe forty-five minutes before Jim was standing directly in front of and above a scraggly old prospector with an even more scraggly burrow loaded to the max. This old boy had been up in the hills panning for gold in tiny streams when he wasn't digging in some hole in the side of a desolate mountain. It was time for him to come back into civilization, which he largely detested, to buy grub, supplies and some whiskey. He'd pay for it with those tiny flakes of gold and those few small nuggets he had collected since his last visit.

"He acknowledged the tall stranger on the saloon porch, but with not much more than maybe a nod. It was then that he made his mistake. He turned to the gunfighter with a sudden motion reaching for his bandanna in his back pocket. It turned out to be a fatal mistake. The sun was in Jim Leslie's eyes so he couldn't see all that was there, and with sharpened reflexes, he drew his weapons of mass destruction. It was over in seconds. A gruesome scene. Twelve shots were fired...most of them hitting the old man in the stomach, thighs and back as he twisted around to the ground. Only then did Jim Leslie realize what he had done. He had gunned down an unarmed man. Jim saw that the dying man had a few breaths left in him so he kneeled down and, cupping his filthy head in his hand said, "Old Timer, I am truly sorry that I killed you. I thought you was making a play and I had no choice but to protect myself. It looks like you're done for, but I got an idea. This here place ain't got no name...tell you what, I'll see to it that we name it after you. What's your name?"

"With that the old man looked up and with his last breath said in a loud voice, "You ma...you ma!" Then he died.

BILLY JOHNSON SCORES AGAIN

Billy went back to the craps table, this time he lost $2.50 very quickly and came back to tell another story. First he ordered a large beer and a shot of Jack. He took a couple of large sips of brew and then dropped the shot glass into the beer. With two gulps he was through the beer and one more gulp through the Jack. He never winced.

"You boys ever hear that expression about a woman bein' 'coyote ugly'? Everyone agreed they had not heard it except an old man at the end of the bar. No one was sure he even heard the question, "Well, here's how it goes: "This here feller was a real lady's man...he got a different gal every night...had quite a stable of fillies who thought right highly of him and couldn't wait to lie with him...he was that good!

"One night he was drinkin' and dancin'...one gal after another. After considerable drinkin' he took one of them ladies to her room. After bumpin' around in bed for an hour or so, he fell asleep just knowin' he had done right smart by her.

"In the mornin' he woke up with blurred vision and a monstrous headache. He looked over at the woman he had bedded and, even with blurred vision, realized that he had his right arm around the most truly ugly lady in the western part of America! She looked like she had recently kissed a train! After thinkin' about his condition, he began to do what coyotes sometimes do when they's caught in a trap. Rather than wake her, he chewed off his arm!"

Lots of laughter went up for the telling of that tale, one man toasted "Here's to coyote ugly!"

About that time a pretty young waitress from the hotel restaurant came in the bar and hearing those words asked, "What's this 'coyote ugly' business...every coyote I ever saw was beautiful?" With that, almost as if it were set up beforehand, Billie began a verse that went like this:

"Coyote ugly" mused the girl with the sil'vry curl
"Whatever could that mean?
"I've looked on coyotes with beautiful coats
"They make a magnificent scene!"

"I will tell you, my friend," said a one-armed man
"Compelled, offered advice.
"You really should see how that phrase came to be
"You will learn that term is not nice!

"It appeared a young man had a one night stand,
"On waking realized
"The beast sleeping there with the thin, graying hair
"Was something he sure could despise!

"He turned and found her, his right arm around her
"Caught! Could not get away!
"As trapped coyotes oft do, he started to chew
"Was freed to love another day.

"Had she been shaken...accident'ly awakened
"My life...changed for the worse.
"Though I have but one arm...no cause for alarm.
"Coyote Ugly's truly a curse!"

Full round of applause with some laughter was offered up for Billy and his well-told verse. The young girl was not applauding nor was she amused. She asked, "What do you think, Jim, is there a clever story and verse for the poor girl who winds up in the same situation...in bed with some greasy, sweathog of a man?"

"I could try it...switchin' roles, but I don't think it'd work.

Some stories are best left the way they was told," said Jim going back to the craps table for another chance at Lady Luck.

❦

BAR MUSIC

The bartender at the Bucket of Blood Saloon in Virginia City, Don Peterson, was proud of his workplace. Some considered the saloon with its Tiffany lamps, ancient back bar and vintage slot machines a national treasure. What he was most pleased with was the little band that played on weekends. There in the back end of the saloon overlooking six mile canyon was an old upright piano, a well-used banjo and a beat up saxophone. The band was on a break after playing an extended set of tunes designed to cause patrons to lift those glasses and pull those slot handles.

Whatever was going on at the Bucket of Blood was working. It was a favorite of the tourists that flooded the city and was quite popular with the locals.

There had been a parade that day... there always seemed to be a parade...a bagpipe group had annoyed the Saturday afternoon tourists and largely had kept them out of the 'Bucket' for half an hour or so. They were drifting back.

During that time a man came into the bar and sat down on one of the rickety bar stools and motioned to Don to come over.

"Mac, I've got my pet with me and I'll bet you a beer that he can play any one of those instruments up on that bandstand."

"Let me get this straight," said Don. "You have an animal in that bucket you're carrying that can play any musical instrument over there?"

10

"Yep, and I'll bet you a beer on it!"

"You're on," said the barkeep.

With that settled, the man opened the lid on his bucket, reached down into the water and pulled out an octopus that, if stretched out completely, would cover the better part of six or seven feet.

A small crowd had gathered after hearing the wager. The man collected his pet and took him over to the piano, sat him upright on the padded stool and walked back to his seat at the bar. Nothing happened for quite a spell, then the octopus, who was named Larry, reached out with all eight tentacles and jumped on Scott Joplin's "The Entertainer's Rag" with confidence and considerable skill. The crowd was taken with this and interrupted frequently with whistles and applause.

As Don poured a draft for the man, he commented, "That's the damndest thing I ever saw...here's your beer."

The crowd placed their orders and gathered around the octopus who had finished his piece and was put back in the bucket of water.

"Bet he can't play that sax," shouted one of the crowd to the pet owner.

"It'll cost you a brew."

"I'll cover that," said a red faced man as he slammed half a beer.

The man went to the bandstand with his pet and placed him near the saxaphone. He stood there for a moment then walked confidently back to his place at the bar.

Again, nothing happened immediately, but when it did it was magnificent! Larry got his fingering on the valves of the sax just right and played "Yackety Sax" better than Boots Randolph ever did. Then he played it again.

A lady in jeans and a western shirt and hat clamored, "Hey

man, I'm bettin' a six pack that your friend here can't play nothin' on that banjo sittin' there!"

The man didn't answer immediately, rather, he sipped his beer thoughtfully and responded, "Larry must be tired by now, but I think he has enough in him to play a tune on the banjo, sure, I'll take you up on it."

After placing Larry by the banjo and returning to his seat, Larry went to his work with a new found energy. He played "Dixie" so well and with such feeling the woman in the western attire brushed away several tears. Larry was returned to his mobile home.

Just then one of the bagpipe players from the recently finished parade came in, put his instrument on the floor and ordered a bourbon and water. A man standing near by brought him up to speed on what was going on. No sooner had the small crowd spied the bagpipe than one of them shouted, "I'll bet a case of Coors that Larry can't play that there thing!"

"OK," said the octopus owner, "but this will have to be the end of it. Larry is tired—let him rest a little in his bucket, I got to get Larry back to his tank pretty soon!"

After a while the man gently picked up his friend and took him over to where the kilted Scotsman was seated.

"Do you mind?" he asked.

The Scotsman nodded approval and disbelief at the same time and watched as the owner placed Larry next to the bagpipe and walked away.

What happened next was the most ferocious fighting, wrestling, squeezing, twisting, end over end commotion ever seen in the Bucket of Blood up to that time. Don Peterson had never seen anything quite like it and began to worry that someone might get hurt.

"OK, OK, that's enough! It's obvious that your octopus can't play a bagpipe. Why don't you settle up your bet and give your friend a rest," directed the bartender.

"Just wait a minute, just a minute," suggested the man, "Soon as Larry figures out he can't screw that thing...he'll play it!"

ở

THREE'S COMPANY

After the octopus had wrestled with it, our bagpipe player, dusted off the cherished musical instrument...called "Grace"... and lovingly deflated it, folded it, and carried it back to his car parked down below the main street. One stop remained, to pick up a CD for a friend and then home. He drove down the twisty, scary road from Virginia City on to Highway 395 toward Reno and turned off at Meadowwood Circle. He parked the old Buick station wagon in the huge parking lot and locked all the doors; but didn't like the prospect of leaving his beloved bagpipe unprotected.

In "Sam Goody's," after browsing a little, our man purchased the CD "Bagpipe Favorites Through the Years" with a special rendition of "Amazing Grace" by the famous "Glasgow Bagpipe Troupe."

On the way back to his car he was still concerned that someone might have broken in and broken his heart.

From a distance he could see his car and from that same distance the broken window was obvious. He rushed to his old car and, looking into the station wagon through the broken window, saw something to break his heart even more. There next to "Grace" lay two more bagpipes!

PERSISTENCE

Don Peterson had no sooner ushered the man and his octopus out the door than a large man came in the door, sat down and ordered a scotch and water. Don could see that the tall stranger was looking a little nervous so he motioned to one of the waitresses to see to his needs.

"What'll it be, Mister?" asked Sylvia.

"Ahm looking for a little action, if you know what I mean," stated the man.

"Tell me what you got, then maybe I can suggest a way to fix you up," directed Sylvia.

"Ah want a woman to give me aid and comfort for the evening," the man retorted.

"What would you have to offer such a woman, that is, if I knew of such a woman who could help you with your needs?"

"Well, Ahm from Texas and Ah have three oil wells pumping as we speak."

"And what else do you have, Stranger?"

"Ah have three cars. One is a new Cadillac, one is a new Lexus, and the other is a new Rolls Royce."

"And what else?"

"Ah have three thousand dollars in my pocket."

"Listen Mister, all that sounds impressive, but personally, what could you offer a working girl?"

"Ah could offer her three inches!"

"Ha!...She would cough and that little feller would jump out!" Sylvia chuckled.

"Yep, it might," the tall stranger smiled, "but she'd have to have the whooping cough to keep it out!"

THE WIND BENEATH...THE BAR!

Don Peterson had the authority to terminate employees if they created situations that, in his opinion, were too risqué. He asked Sylvia to find someplace else to work and asked the tall stranger from Texas to leave the "Bucket."

About that time a distinguished man and his wife came in, played slot machines for a spell, then sat at the bar and ordered gin and tonics. Don struck up a conversation with the couple and learned that they were from London and were visiting the American west. They had flown into San Franciso, visited the wine region, gold country, Carson City, Reno and now were touring Virginia City. They were having a wonderful time!

Just then, Paul Pager, a year round resident of Virginia City, sat down near them, ordered a beer and, on taking a sip, released a very loud, obnoxious and lengthy volume of gas.

The demeanor of the Briton changed from one of jovial tourist to one of wounded, cultured gentleman. He looked at Paul with disgust and said, "How dare you break wind before my wife!"

Paul, looking straight ahead said, "I'm sorry sir, I didn't know it was her turn!"

15

CORRECTION

Benny Worthy was always the class fool, a nerd. Somehow he had managed to get a girlfriend during the last part of his senior year at Virginia City High School. She was quite a catch...Barbra Sue. Never had the charm or intelligence to collect a bevy of interested boys. She could not have done better than Benny and Benny probably could not have done worse than Barbra Sue.

Somehow they found comfort in each other. Benny was always trying to prove to himself and to his two older brothers, that he was their equal. But, alas, he wasn't.

Benny had finished high school and was very interested in going to the University of Nevada at Las Vegas. He had heard that they had a good English Department and he had decided to get a degree in that subject in hopes of teaching at VC High later on.

Barbra Sue had no such interest or abilities and on getting out of high school got a full-time job in the 'Candy Factory' on main street in VC.

Benny went to Las Vegas, lived on campus and never came home once during two semesters. When his first year was over, he took an afternoon flight to Reno where Barbra Sue met him and drove him up to Virginia City.

After dinner at his folks home, Benny and Barbra Sue took her car up to Boot Hill Cemetery for a little serious making out. It was a very dark night, no moon, no stars and the occasional howl of a distant coyote.

After lots of smooching, groping, fondling and other things... nothing too serious, mind you, Barbra Sue, catching her breath and looking around at the tombstones and moonless sky, commented, "Gee, ain't it gruesome!" Benny, full of two semesters of bonehead English at the University of Nevada at Las Vegas, replied in a condescending tone, "Barbra Sue, what you should have said was Gee, hasn't it grown some!"

ॐ

A SIGN OF THE TIMES

It was a slow night at Bernice's Ranch brothel in Elko when the buzzer sounded and all the girls came to attention. Bernice answered by grabbing a quick look out the window and seeing no staggering drunk, no Boston-Strangler look-a-like, no young boys or butch-looking women, she pushed her button opening the gate. The man came in, looked over the crowd, looked to Bernice and beckoned her to a corner of the double wide trailer.

"Madam," he said with emphasis, "I've been to cat houses in every part of this great nation of ours and to most of the better whore houses in Nevada. Frankly, Madam, I am bored with what I see at most of these places and with all of what I do at these places."

"Well, what the hell do you want?" Bernice responded... and quickly.

"I want something different, do you know what I mean?"

"No, sir, I do not know what you mean!" Bernice shot back.

"I've done the deed in about every position you've ever heard of or seen...I've had sex standing, sitting, kneeling, both facing south, both facing each other, one south...one north, just name it, I've done it!" he said in one long breath.

"Maybe then, what you need is to look at different

17

locations," she smiled.

"Yes, but you have to understand that I've screwed in the bedroom, kitchen, bathroom, on the floor, on the patio, in my car, in her car, in a borrowed car, a truck, a van, on top of a van... name it!" he smiled.

"You say you took your pleasure on top of a van? How about on top of a whore house?" she queried.

"You know, I never have. Can you arrange that?" he asked.

"I sure can, but it will take a few minutes. Oh, by the way, that will cost you $250," she quietly extorted.

"$250, why so much...oh, never mind..." grumbling as he handed her three hundreds, receiving a crisp fifty quick as a wink.

It wasn't long before our gentleman and his lady were naked and on the gently sloping roof really getting it on. In the heat of true passion, and paying a little mind to that earlier mentioned gentle sloping roof, the two began to roll...once... twice...then a short fall into some sagebrush and tumbleweeds that had blown up against the trailer. They never missed a beat.

A very drunk cowboy standing at the gate and observing this entire matter pushed the buzzer with urgency. Bernice answered, "Cowboy, you're too drunk to come in here. Why don't you go get sobered up and come back?"

The cowboy thought for a moment and responded, "I don't want to come in. I just want to tell you your sign fell down."

SO WHAT'S THE PROBLEM?

The Elko County Court House was in the center of interest among the town's people that cold September morning. It was the first day of the trial that had captured the interest of everyone east of Battle Mountain. The trial had even been noticed by papers in Reno and Salt Lake City. The case centered around what today would be called bestiality, yes, that's right...the "B" word! It seems that a woman named Mary Ruth Shirley had unintentionally observed a sheep herder named Rico Dagnello performing a sex act with a sheep. The jury had been picked and this was the opening day for the prosecution's chief, and only witness against Dagnello. Mary Ruth was on the stand.

"Now, Mary Ruth, I want you to tell the jury exactly what you saw that late afternoon near Jigs, Nevada."

After a moment composing herself, Mary Ruth replied, "I saw a man look at a small flock of sheep, pick out one of them and drag it into some tall sagebrush nearby."

"Miss Shirley, is that man in this courtroom today?"

"Yes, he's sittin' over there," she pointed to the defendant.

"Please tell the jury what happened next," directed the lawyer, one Justin P. Young, an Assistant District Attorney who came from Boise, Idaho several years before. Justin viewed this trial and the certain conviction as his ticket to Carson City and who-knows-what after service in the Nevada legislature.

"He put the left rear leg of that sheep in his left boot," she replied, holding back a little grin.

"Now, Miss Shirley, tell this court exactly what happened next," replied Mr. Young, acting perhaps a little over-confident.

"He then put the right rear leg of the ewe in his right boot and unzipped his pants," she replied, this time expressionless. "This is extremely important, Miss Shirley. I want you to tell everyone in this courtroom what happened next."

"It was the strangest thing...the sheep turned around and licked that man on the hand," she replied curiously.

With that comment, one of the jurors, a crusty old rancher from the Wendover area, whispered to a fellow juror, also a rancher, "They'll do that sometimes!"

❦

A NICE NOTE

Justin Young, Elko's Assistant District Attorney, and soon to be the county's newest assemblyman, even though he had lost his last case involving a man having sex with a sheep, had one more case to try before he headed off to Carson City for the opening of the legislative session. The case involved a woman who had been attacked and sexually assaulted by a near-do-well drifter from Winnemucca. He was apprehended quickly and thus the reason for the trial.

The woman, a lady named Beth Grissom from Jarbidge, Nevada was on the witness stand and Assistant District Attorney Young was quizzing her.

"Mrs. Grissom, do you see the man who attacked you in this courtroom?"

"Yes sir, he is," and pointed to the tall non-descript looking man sitting by the defense counsel.

"Your honor, let the record show that my client has pointed to the defendant, Mr. Claiborne Sticks," directed Mr. Young. The judge so ordered.

"Mrs. Grissom, will you please tell the court exactly what Mr. Sticks said to you just before he attacked you. That is, as best you can remember, the exact conversation that took place."

"I'm afraid I can't repeat what he said...it was so awful!" pleaded the witness.

"Come now, Mrs. Grissom, we are all adults and it will be necessary, if we are to put this man behind bars, that you tell this court what he said he was going to do to you," chided Mr. Young.

"I just can't repeat what he said, I'm sorry," the distraught woman replied.

"Your honor, would it be permissible for my client to write down what her attacker said. We could then circulate her note to the jurors."

The judge agreed and it wasn't very long before Mrs. Grissom handed the bailiff a slip of paper which he gave to the juror on the end.

Each juror read the note with disgust passing it on to the next. One very pretty young lady blushed, but quickly passed it to the rancher who was sitting next to her. Unbeknownst to her, the rancher had been dozing through much, no, all of the proceedings and when she shook him and passed the note he read it, turned to her, smiled, winked and put the note in his pocket.

❧

APPARENTLY NOT

A dusty old prospector out in the hills above Tuscarora, Nevada in the early days happened upon an old Indian laid out

21

on the trail ahead of him. The miner approached the Indian very cautiously. He had heard about Indians ambushing people and stealing everything they had. He had his hand on his gun and was ready for anything the Indian might come up with.

As he approached, he could see the Indian was dazed but unkilled and there apparently were no consorts laying in wait for him and, after a brief word or two, the injured man gave the following account of his troubles.

"With my ear to the ground like this I can hear the big wheels of a Conestoga wagon carrying the treasure of an early settler and his family moving west along this rocky trail. The family consisted of a middle aged man, his wife wearing a big bonnet, and six children...four boys and two girls... all weary and ready to make camp after a long day's ride over some of the roughest land in all the Nevada territory. The two oxen have very heavy hooves and kick up a lot of dust as they pull the heavily laden wagon."

The miner was curious that he had found such an articulate red man so far from civilization, which would be Elko, some 95 miles away. He asked, "You can tell all that just by puttin' your ear to the ground?"

"Hell no, you fool," shouted the Indian, "It just so happens that not more than half an hour ago they ran over my ass!"

COMMUNICATIONS

It happened near Wells.

It was the early days all right, Nevada was still a territory. The most important man alive was none other than the Lone

Ranger. He had been in Elko County for some time now and he was beating up on the local outlaws and crooks for almost a year and things were going pretty good for the county. One morning while riding Silver half way between Wells and Elko, looking for ways to do good, correct injustice and generally advance law and order, he was set upon by a band of renegade Indians. Silver managed to escape, but the masked man was savaged pretty good. While they didn't exactly skin him alive...that was being done by Indians of another tribe back east...they stripped him of his handsome outfit, whipped him plenty with rawhide strips, stole all his silver bullets, and kicked his ass with gusto. When they'd had about all the fun they intended to have, they soaked those rawhide leather strips in the creek that ran nearby and stretched them good. They then tied several strips around his neck, hands, and feet, and staked him out spread eagle, knowing full well that when the sun dried the leather it would shrink back to the original length and nothing could stop it. That meant the Lone Ranger would be agonizingly choked to death and probably eaten by coyotes later that day.

After a brief display of high-pitched hollering and shouting, the Indians tore out for the Ruby Marshes with their booty. After a spell, the unmasked man regained consciousness and looking through battered and swollen eyes, could see Silver prancing around on a little hill about 200 yards away.

"Silver...come here," he shouted, but which amounted to little more than table conversation pitch.

With that, Silver reared up and gave his best whinny and charged down the slope, hopping over the little stream, coming to a snorting halt just before trampling all over the outstretched, choking Kimosabe. Silver leaned all the way over and received a brief, whispered, directive from the ranger. He then lit out in the direction of Elko easily over twenty-five miles west.

Hours passed, lots of them. The Lone Ranger could feel the necklace tightening to the point of losing consciousness many times. Breaths came rapidly but they kept coming. Maybe it was five hours, maybe it was six hours, who knows? The sun was relentless, the dry desert wind acted like a sandblasting machine. Then, he looked over to the knoll and could see his great white stallion prancing around on that same hill. It looked like Silver was carrying a naked woman riding side saddle with long blond hair blowing in that dry desert wind. With what he thought might be his last breath, but wasn't, the ranger shouted, "Silver, come here."

Again, Silver reared up...nearly throwing his naked passenger...gave another most excellent whinny and charged down the slope, hopping over the little stream and, again, nearly stepping all over the lawman.

The Lone Ranger whispered, "Silver, closer, closer," Silver leaned way over and put his ear to his master's parched lips. "Silver, Damn it! I said 'POSSE'!!!"

THE WEST—WHERE THE REAL MEN LIVE

It was a hot, windy day that turned into a hot windy night as three cowpokes sat around a campfire in Northern Elko County just outside a dusty little town called Tuscarora. The three had finished a monotonous day of rounding up cows, a fair amount of branding new additions to the herd, and a lot of bouncing atop shiny leather saddles. They had a basic meal of beans, salt pork, and hardtack, washed down with several cups of strong black coffee. One of the cowboy's broke out a bottle of "Who Shot John?" which was passed around until most of it, no, all of it, was history.

The subject of their conversation evolved into who was the strongest, bravest, wisest, most fearless cowhand in the territory. "I'm tough, I'm rough," exclaimed a young man in his late twenties...they called him Jim. "Just the other day, I was ridin' up near Jarbridge and a mountain lion jumped on my back and began killin' me. He was bitin' and clawin' and I could feel myself gettin' all bloody and hurting real bad. I figured I was goin' under, but I had one more thing I was gonna do before I did. I reached around and run my fist down the lion's throat, grabbed him by his asshole and turned him inside out...then I threw his carcass into a pile of sagebrush nearby." He sat down convinced that his tale would not be bettered.

Terrence, a man in his early thirties, but looking much older, got up from the log he was sitting on, added a few sticks to the fire and said something to the effect that Jim's story, though somewhat supportive of the bragging, was nothing compared to what he had been through. He lit his pipe using a flaming twig, drew deeply and commenced, "Last month I was ridin' near Mountain City out by that thicket of quakin' aspens when a huge boa constrictor come out of the Quakies and wrapped himself around me and started to tighten and tighten and tighten. I could feel my very life bein' squeezed outta my body. I just knew I was done for when I thought of something. I reached around and grabbed his head with one hand and unwrapped him with the other, skinned him with my teeth and ate him like an ear of corn. I realized I was one of the meanest and toughest men north of the Humboldt River."

Some time passed before the third cowboy stood up. When he did, he didn't speak. He simply unzipped his pants and began stirring the coals of the fire with his dick.

❦

OPENING NIGHT

There had been several very nice restaurants in Carson City over the years, but only a few of them had staying ability. One such restaurant, Adela's, had taken up residence in an old house on Carson Street and was famous for atmosphere and fine food, but there was more room in this growing northern Nevada community for haut cuisine. Thomas Pryor was just the man to bring great food and greater prices to Carson.

He set out and found the best location, bought the best furniture (carpets, wall coverings, paintings...all oil...natch!), installed perfect lighting, table settings found only in the finest mansions in Europe, crystal stemware, fresh flowers, the finest food and just the right music. Yes, the music had to be perfection. To that end he had built a raised platform in the middle of the dining room and bought a shiny new Steinway grand piano for the entertainment. Everything, he thought, was now perfect.

After placing numerous advertisements in the 'Nevada Appeal' for a piano player and getting only drunks and misfits as applicants, Thomas was getting discouraged. The restaurant, his dream, was almost ready for the grand opening, but he had not filled that important niche. Days went by, interviews and tryouts produced nothing.

One afternoon he was summoned from the kitchen by one

of his staff and introduced to a middle aged man named Robert Peck. Let me describe Robert. Tall, slender, blue jeans (with knees showing thru), torn pockets, worn chambray shirt, untrimmed beard, John Lennon glasses, and of course, a pony tail.

Thomas sized him up and, being busy, tried to dispatch him by saying, "I'm sorry the position has already been filled."

"Sir, I wish you would just listen to my music. I'm sure you will find a place for me, if not now, then maybe later on," responded Robert.

"OK, but quickly, my time is short and I am expecting a player from Reno in 15 minutes," said Mr. Pryor.

With that, Robert stepped up to the piano and began playing the most haunting melody Thomas had ever heard. After four minutes he was nearly crying because the song was so captivating.

When Robert had finished, he looked over to Thomas who was brushing away a tear and said, "Well, sir, what do you think?"

"I'm impressed, my God! I'm very impressed. What, by the way, was the name of that tune? I don't think I have ever heard anything quite like it."

"That is one of my own compositions... in fact... I write all my own music."

"How interesting, but what was the name of that piece?"

"I call it, 'My Dick Is So Long I Can Slap The Back Of My Neck With It.'"

Thomas Pryor was taken aback. After he gained his composure, he said, "Robert, here's what I'm offering. I'm excited about your music. Here, I'll advance you $500 to get a suit or two, a good shave and haircut, some nice shoes and be ready for opening night this Saturday. Oh, by the way Robert, just play your music...you don't ever tell anybody the names of your songs. Do you understand?"

After an enthusiastic "OK," Robert headed off to do his shopping.

Saturday night came, the place was booked solid for all three seatings and things could not be going smoother or better. The dining room was beautiful, the food was superb, and the music, well, the music was outstanding. Robert's tip jar was emptied several times during the evening.

Thomas was pleased with the way things were going. He walked over to the piano area and congratulated Robert with a pat on the back commenting and asking, "Your music is beautiful, Robert, what was the name of that last piece you played?"

"That one was named, 'My Butt Hair Is So Long I Can Braid It Into A Belt!'"

Thomas shuddered a little and repeated his caveat about not ever mentioning the names of any of his songs to the guests.

The evening progressed and the music just kept getting better and better. Finally, Robert took a needed break and went to the men's room, but in his haste to return to his music he forgot to zip up his pants. When he returned to the dias he launched into his most favored work with elegance, beauty and skill.

He noticed that the elderly couple sitting to his right, while enthralled with his performance, kept looking at him with some discomfort. When the song was finished the nicely dressed silver-haired lady sitting there commented, "We are enjoying your music ever so much son, but do you know your penis and your testicle are hanging out?"

"Know it? Know it? Robert shouted with joy, "I wrote it!"

❧

BEAR IN MIND

There are few bears in Nevada, but there are some. Mostly in the Sierra Mountains that border part of the state. I have seen a mother and two cubs one time...they went one way and I went the other out of mutual respect, I suppose.

This is the story about the Carson City man who went bear hunting near Topaz Lake. He was in a well concealed blind on a bluff overlooking an area where he had seen bear tracks earlier. Hours passed then suddenly he saw a huge bear behind a log. The bear roared defiance...sensing a human was in the area. As he reared up, our Carson man let go with his best shot. Down went the bear.

It took some time for our guy to work his way down the hillside and over through the brush to the log. He searched and searched, but he found no bear. Suddenly, he felt a tap on his shoulder and as he turned, he found himself looking right in the face of this huge brown bear.

"I'll give you two choices," said the bear. "Choice 'A' is that I will tear you to pieces, slowly, limb by limb! Choice 'B' is I will sexually ravish you, but will leave you alive... what'll it be?"

The man thought for a brief moment and realizing in a Hobson's choice none of the choices is very good, selected "B."

When the bear was finished with our Carson chap, he went on his way. The man, more dead than alive, could think of only one thing...to go back to Carson City and after he recovered sufficiently, buy a bigger gun and come back to this very spot.

It took about a week, but our man found himself in the best gun shop in Carson City where he bought a huge gun. The store keeper confirmed that this piece would drop the biggest bear in his tracks.

Back to the Topaz area...back to the blind...waiting, waiting! Then, there he was...yes! It had to be the same bear...there was something about him. He raised his gun, fired, saw the bear drop behind the log and made his way down to collect his trophy. A panic set in...there was no bear...then a tap on the shoulder.

"What'll it be, man...'A' or 'B'? The man chose 'B' again and endured the ravishing as best he could. Later when he was back in that Carson City gun shop, he knew what he had to do.

"I want a bazooka. I not only want to kill me a bear, I want to blow him to tiny pieces," said the man to the salesman.

Back to Topaz, back to the blind, and yes, as he saw the bear raising up behind the same log, he got the bear in the cross hairs of the bazooka and fired. The bear dropped like a hot rock. As he quickly ran down the embankment across the little meadow over to the log, he expected only to see bits and pieces of what used to be a bear. But, you guessed it, no bear anywhere to be found.

There was a tap on his shoulder and as he turned, the bear looked him curiously in the eye and said, "You're not in this for the hunting are you?"

❦

COMFORT STATION

Did you ever wonder how the expression "Well, how about that!" got started? Here is the true story.

Fort Churchill Captain Jim Bucks, had his men out chasing some renegade Indians about twenty miles from the fort when night fell. He thought it best if he could put his men up in some of the surrounding homes, barns, etc. as it looked like it might rain. He came to a house and summoned the owner out.

"I'm Captain Bucks and I need a place to billet my men for the night. How many can you take?" he asked with a slow Texas drawl.

"Captain, I am heartily sorry, but my small home is already full of visitors from Ely, but I could take one of your men. He would be welcome to sleep in the small barn...at least he would be dry," said the owner.

"Thank you, sir," and with that the Captain turned and ordered, "Corporal Peters, fall out and remain here tonight. We will be back to pick you up at 0700 tomorrow."

Down the dusty road the captain lead his troops until he came upon a larger ranch. He ordered his sergeant to go fetch the owner.

"Ma'am, I need to find some comfort for my men tonight. It's been a long day and they would appreciate your help this evening," said the Captain.

What the Captain from Texas did not know was that he was talking to the Madam of the Salt Flats brothel. Vivian Lane had operated the house for nearly three years, coming from Reno.

"How many men do you have here?" asked Vivian.

"Ma'am, there are 59 men without Peters," said Captain Bucks.

To which the Madam said, "Well, how about that!"

❦

NAP TIME!

The Famous Mustang Ranch, located some 12 miles east of Reno in Storey County has been the source of many stories over the years. One of the most famous yarns involves a 92 year old man visiting the ranch one spring evening.

"What can I do you for?" asked the Madam on duty.

"I want to have a drink and then I want one of your best girls...a blond will do nicely," returned the well-dressed gentleman.

"You're serious, aren't you, Pop?" inquired the shift manager.

"You bet, I'm serious. Don't think that just because there is snow on the roof there's no fire in the basement!" was his trite reply.

"You have your drink and I'll send some ladies over for company."

The man ordered and received his gin and tonic, paid his $10.00, and grumbled to the barkeep who responded by rote, "On your way in, sir, did you happen to see a sign advertising 'Mustang Bar'? We have a happy hour, but it's back in one of the cribs, not out here!"

"I deserved that," returned the senior citizen as he toasted the bartender. Darleen Rose, the manager-madam returned with two blondes tagging along.

"I want you to meet Ramona and Ginger. They told me

they would be delighted to have a date with you. Why don't you have a cocktail and go have some fun?" Darleen departed and the ladies sat on either side of the man.

"Thanks, but I don't need any more booze and I don't need two ladies to do what I have in mind. Ginger, let's go," directed our gentleman.

Ginger lead the man rather quickly to a small room with a sink and double bed with mirrors everywhere. After he told her what he wanted to do and she extracted $65.00 from him... leaving the room to deposit the money someplace... she returned and the trick began.

For the working girl it was a very good trick. The old man knew what he was doing and he was good at it. All in all, Ginger was quite pleased with their experience and she started a little conversation with him afterwards.

It seems that the man had been an athlete in his earlier days and had kept in good shape all his life. He worked out frequently, took vitamins, ate the right things and, generally looked thirty years younger than his age. Ginger felt drawn to him, and seeing that Tuesdays were usually slow made him an offer he just couldn't turn down.

"Pops, tell you what. If you can do what you just did one more time, I won't charge you."

"I'll take you up on that, and thank you. By the way, there is one thing I will ask you to do, however, and that is to take both your hands and hold on to my penis while I take about a 10 minute nap. That's about the only way I can do this," offered the man, feeling this might kill her offer.

"OK by me!" was her immediate and pleased response.

She did and he did and, in about ten minutes, the old man woke up with renewed vigor and proceeded to give her the thrill she only got with her boyfriend in Reno on those nights she wasn't working.

"Hey, Daddy!" Ginger exclaimed nearly exhausted. "Let's do that again! You are the best trick I've ever turned. Tell you what... if you can do that again, I'll give you your money back. What a man!! You are definitely going to have to be a regular!"

"Suits me, but you know the drill. You'll have to hold onto my penis with both hands while I take a little nap... about 10 minutes."

"Let's go!" Ginger said eagerly.

To tell the truth, Ginger needed time to recover from the previous workout. When the man awoke, he dedicated himself to fulfilling her every wish and desire. She experienced those things women don't always experience during these kinds of activities. When the two were finished Ginger was exhilarated, but exhausted. She stayed on the bed panting while our man dressed himself then commented, "Dad, you're quite a man! I'm so glad you picked me tonight. Can you call for me next time you're here. Better yet, why don't we set up an out-call at your place?" She gave him one of her cards. *"Ginger Spice" Hostess, Mustang Ranch* and her phone and fax number.

"But, Pops, would you tell me one thing? What's the deal with my holding your joint while you take a nap? What's happening there?"

"Oh, that's nothing," replied the man straightening his tie. "The last girl stole my wallet!"

COMMUNICATIONS 101

It was France during the middle part of the Second World War. The allies were making slow progress; casualties were moderate as expected.

The latest batch of conscripts was from northern California and Nevada. Two such "volunteers" were Paiute Indians from the Pyramid Lake reservation near Reno. They spoke some, but not very much English.

After numerous briefings by captains and sergeants, the two soldiers along with two hundred other troops assigned from other parts of the front line were stationed in a bunker not more than 200 yards from the enemy. Plans called for a late afternoon charge that was sure to be successful. All military intelligence (oxymoron) indicated the Germans would be caught with their knickerbockers down and would rout easily.

The time came and the order was given to "Charge!"

Out they went! Rifles at the ready, it was a glorious thing. Soldiers on the right and left were dropping, there was screaming also, and loud shouts for "medic!" Then a loud mortar went off between the two Indians and they separated quickly. One Indian, a boy name "Wolf," dove for a deep hole created moments earlier and still warm.

Seconds later, a very large soldier crowded in and held his head low. The shelling stopped for a few minutes and the big guy tried to start up a conversation. Nothing he said registered and there was no response. He then thought he would try some sign language and began by, "Soldier, are you in the paratroopers?" he asked, lowering his wiggling fingers trying to simulate parachute.

35

The Indian looked interested in this effort, but did not respond.

"Are you in the infantry?" asked the big guy walking his fingers up his arm.

Nothing.

"Are you in the armament division?" quizzed the soldier grasping his right bicep and moving his forearm upward with a clenched fist.

The big man noticed that the little guy took on a look of terror, but he did not say anything.

"Are you in reconnaissance?" asked the soldier. This would be his last inquiry. With the question, he made circles with his thumb and index fingers and brought them to his eyes like binoculars.

With that, and without a word, the little guy jumped out of the ditch and started running and dodging mortars that had begun anew. He found his way to where his buddy was crouching. His pal shouted in their native language, "Wolf, what are you doing, you could have been killed out there."

"I could have gotten worse over in that ditch! This big guy got in there with me and told me this." He began by doing the parachute number. Wolf's pal commented, "He said, 'When the sun goes down...'"

Wolf shook his head in agreement. Then he walked his fingers up his arm. His buddy quickly said, "...and all the troops have gone away..."

Wolf then made a fist, bent his arm up and grabbed his bicep—his friend gasped—then Wolf put his circled fingers to his eyes—his buddy in disbelief said, "He told you he was going to screw you until your eyes bugged out!"

❦

THE OUTFIT

There was excitement, lots of it...and there were pretty girls, lots of them. They were attracted to the cowboys at the Elko rodeo and the cowboys were too busy doing rodeo things to pay them much more than lustful gawks.

TV station KNNV had sent a team to Elko to measure the excitement at this rodeo and had set up an interview station overlooking the stadium. A young, beautiful lady with microphone in hand was telling the camera that she was at the Elko Rodeo, commented on the great weather, the crowd, and a lot more about the cowboys. After a brief opening, she called to a young man named Harry Tesh, who had been waiting off-camera. Harry walked over kicking up dust a little.

"This is Harry Tesh, he's been calf roping and bronco riding on the rodeo circuit for three years now. Harry, maybe you can tell our viewers about the outfit you're wearing."

"Glad to, Ma'am. This wide hat I'm wearin' keeps the sun off my face and when I'm in competition, I hold it high and slap my horse's rump with it. That sometimes gets me extra points."

"What about your bandana?" asked Shelly Landry.

"This red checked bandana goes around my neck for sun protection and to keep dirt outta my shirt. I sometimes wet it down and it keeps me cool."

"And the shirt?"

"Just a shirt...always long sleeves to protect me from scrapes and sun. Has to be of good quality...those cheap shirts don't hold up. Some fellers put stitchin' all over them but that ain't necessary," said Harry.

"Anything special about your pants?" asked Shelly.

"They are just jeans and we go through a bunch of them each season. Some hold up better than other brands, but usually one season and they are done for."

"And why do you wear boots?"

"We wear boots," said Harry with a smile, "so folks won't think we're truck drivers."

❧

A SIGN OF PEACE?

Fort Churchhill was a well built army outpost near a town called Fallon, Nevada. The main function of this fort was to assure safe passage for the migration of easterners and midwesterners heading west to find gold or settle the land. The fort had several captains over the years and the fort commander post had just been filled with a young lieutenant named Jim Bucks who had come from the pan handle of Texas after being promoted to captain.

Shortly after he arrived at the fort and had inspected the facilities, he mounted his new horse and had the men open the heavy wooden gates for him to go for a short ride outside. There was little danger from Indians that lived in the area.

On his way out he noticed an old Indian sitting near the gate...the two acknowledged each other and the new captain rode to a small hill nearby, scoped the area thoroughly, and returned to the fort, shouting for the sentry to open the gates for him.

Back in his office, the captain summoned the sergeant commenting, "Sarge, I had a pleasant ride just now, but I noticed this old Indian sitting by the front gate and he gave me some odd gestures with his finger. Maybe you know sign language and can explain what those gestures mean."

"I'll try Captain, what gestures did he make?"

The Captain held out his right hand, extended his middle finger and gestured twice in an upward motion. With a slight grin, the sarge broke the news to his captain, "That's easy, sir, that means he don't like you very much. What else did he do?"

Then the captain gestured with his middle finger in a horizontal double motion. "What do you suppose that means, Sarge?"

"Well, sir, that means he don't like your horse either!"

COMPARISONS

Billy Artos was given to hyperbole...comparisons, and an occasional gross exaggeration. As a long time resident of Yerington, Nevada he found most of his material in and around his home town. One time I asked Billy if he had lived all this life in Yerington, he replied, "Not yet."

Billy could run off a string of unlikely events that would make you wonder if they had let him 'out' too soon. For example, if anyone were to ask him how the weather was he could reply, "It's so windy I saw a chicken lay the same egg four times. It's so hot I saw a coyote chasin' a rabbit and they was both walkin! It's hotter than a two dollar pistol, hotter than the hinges of hell. It's so cold, you can pee, it will freeze and still be warm. It's so dry water in the Walker River is only wet on one side! It's cold enough to freeze the balls off a brass monkey, colder than a whore's heart, colder than a well digger's ass, colder than a witch's tit!"

This man from Yerlington could use animals effectively in his descriptions as well. "Why that feller was crazy as a loon. Crazy like a fox, blind as a bat, busy as a bee, stubborn as a mule, had a memory like an elephant, was good at playin' possum, quiet as a mouse, faster than a bat outta hell, but had dogged determination."

I asked him, "Billy, everyone knows you have a quick mind, a quick wit, a funnybone and a toothy grin, but do you have the stomach for a real head game?" Billy responded, "Rick, you know I'm busier than a one armed paperhanger, busier than a three peckered goat and a two dicked weasel. You understand that you'd have as much chance as a one-legged man in an ass-kicking contest.

"OK, Billy, I can see that you're in a blue mood and you look white as a sheet. If we were to play, you'd either be green with envy at my skills or red with rage. There wouldn't be any gray areas...It'd all be black or white, nothing rosy about it. Glad you ain't gonna be a yellow belly."

Something had happened. Billy, whose come-backs were usually faster than a speeding bullet were now slower than molasses in January. Billy, whose retorts were always more slippery than snot on a *door* knob were now deader than a *door* nail. The reason was simple, Billy was drunker than a skunk, higher than a kite, tighter than a tick, smashed, pickled, sloshed, pissed, snockered, toasted, blitzed, hammered, buzzed, juiced, inebriated, intoxicated and feeling no pain cause he was three sheets to the wind!

Just then Billy's wife Melba came in. Melba, who is usually sweeter than pie was cold as ice, appearing meaner than a snake. Here is a lady who most times is cuter than a bug, became colder than a bear's nose. Billy, quicker than a wink, knew he was about to get a knuckle sandwich, she had fist of steel, you know, so he acted quite sheepish, "Why, Melba, when you're mad you're pretty as a picture. You know you're the apple of my eye and I'd give my eye teeth for you!" Billy slurred his words.

"Billy, you snake in the grass! Shut your pie hole! You have a lot of nerve, lot of gall to come in here in your cups after chasin' skirts all day. With that she gave Billy the back of her hand, a smack in the kisser and left the room in a huff quick as a wink!

"Sorry, Billy!" I said. "Call me tomorrow if you need a shoulder to cry on. Try to keep a stiff upper lip. We both know Melba has a good heart, but she's put her ear to the ground and heard through the grapevine you got an eye for the girls and only wants to keep you on your toes—to keep your back to the wall and your nose to the grindstone. Unless you straighten up and fly right, Melba will continue to keep your feet to the fire.

"Good-bye, Rick. I would have liked to match wits with you tonight, but Melba has cooked my goose! In tonight's battle of wits, I'm afraid I'd have been a conscientious objector."

🐮

OIL! FIRE!

Three oil company owners stood on a hill overlooking Railroad Valley in South Central Nevada and shook their heads as they watched a fortune go up in black, thick smoke. After years of funding prospectors, wildcatters, and drillers, they had finally seen a well pumping crude oil in a barren state never known for oil production. Then there was a 'spark' of unknown origin. The raging well-head fire that ensued, moment-by-moment, ate into their avaricious dreams of riches. If not riches, then certainly dreams of paying back their investors and making a little dough of their own. They were flexible.

They had sent urgent telegrams to Red Adair...the consumate well-head fire fighter, but he was busy putting out those same kinds of fires in Kuwait. Fires set by that chief arsonist, Saddam Hussein as he beat it back to Baghdad. None of Red's crew was available or would be available for maybe over a year. What to do?

In desperation, they got word out to a man who trained under Red Adair...a man named Chico Jose Gonzalez...that there would be major bucks if he could get over to Nevada and put this fire out! Major Dinero!

The telegram they received two weeks earlier indicated that Chico Jose Gonzalez would definitely take the assignment and get over to Railroad Valley as quick as he could. They waited and waited.

"Where the hell is that guy?" asked one of the magnates. "Relax," assured the remaining two owners, "he'll be here...his telegram said he was on his way."

Later that morning, word was gotten to the owners that a telegram had arrived in camp that, indeed, Chico Jose Gonzalez was on his way and would be here by noon.

Well, noon came and went...so did one and so did two o'clock. At two-thirty one of the crew shouted.

"Here he comes!" pointing east in the direction of Ely.

All that could be seen was a dust devil shaped cloud and all that could be heard was a mufferless motor vehicle choking, misfiring and belching.

42

Within three minutes, the big shots could make out an old Ford Ranchero loaded with workers bearing down on them going about 85 miles-per-hour. They all had to hustle to clear a path for this out-of-control beater missile.

And scamper they did! They cleared the dusty road just in time to see this worn out Ranchero scream past them, down the hill and go directly into the smoke and fire at the well-head.

"What a guy...what a team, why I'm damned if I ever saw anything like that before! What courage!" marveled the big boss.

Just then there was this earth-shaking explosion completely extinguishing the fire. By the time the owners and reporters from Reno and Las Vegas could make it down the hill, the smoke was clearing and they could see the Ranchero being pushed by a blackened and bruised crew with a small scorched man behind the wheel. As they approached the car, one of the reporters shouted.

"Are you Chico Jose Gonzalez?" The little guy exhaustedly nodded in agreement. "Then you have to be the greatest well-head fire fighter of all times. You will be in demand all over the world! You and your crew are going to be rich beyond your dreams! What's the first thing you're going to do with all the money you just made?"

Chico Jose Gonzalez hesitated for a moment and thoughtfully responded. "The first theeng I weel do with all theese money is to get the focking brakes feexed on theese Ranchero!"

❦

BEAR TALE

Beowawe is a little village you pass at a distance when on your way east between Battle Mountain and Carlin on Interstate 80. An interesting sidelight about Battle Mountain: almost every town in Nevada has its initials drawn and painted on one of its surrounding mountains. Battle Mountain folk put up the letters "B and MT." Right? Wrong! The townspeople put "BM." Don't you think people just riding through the area might wonder why those familiar initials would be put on that mountain?

One night a big black bear wanders into the only bar in this very small town of Beowawe, looks around a little, sits on one of the stools and says, "Bartender, I want a Cuba Libra with a double line."

Well, the bartender doesn't cotton to uppity bears and says, "Stranger, we're fresh out!" hoping the bear would just go away.

"In that case, give me a Singapore Sling with extra fruit."

"Sorry, pal, all out."

"Ok!" says the bear. I want a gin and tonic, lotsa lime...and this time you better come up with it or I'm going to be very pissed!"

Seeing he had gone about as far as he dared with this, the barkeep poured him his drink and said, "That will be ten dollars!"

"Ten dollars? Man that's pricey!" grumbled the bear while he took a sip on his G and T, forking over a ten spot.

The bartender, now feeling as maybe he was a little harsh on the bear, tried to make an apology by way of a little conversation, "Say, big fella, how you doin'? We don't get many bears in here...kinda unusual, know what I mean?"

"No wonder," replied the bear, "you'd get more if you weren't chargin' ten bucks a drink!"

Well, that just about frosted the bartender. He watched as the bear took his drink over to one of the booths and sat quietly sipping.

A little later, the bear, after finishing his cocktail motioned to the bartender to come over.

"This time I want a Miller Genuine Draft," directed the bruin.

"We don't serve beers," said the bartender, "to bears in Beowawe, so you better beat it."

"Let me get this straight. You're a bartender, I'm a bear, this is a bar in Beowawe, and you're telling me you 'don't serve beers to bears in Beowawe and I'd better beat it,' is that what you're saying? Because if that's correct, I'm going to go over there and kill that woman!"

Suspecting a bluff, the bartender repeated his statement, "You heard it buddy, as a bartender in this Beowawe bar...no beers to bears, so beat it!"

The bear jumped up, raced to the lady, devoured her, beer nuts and all and returned to the bartender. A few minutes later, the town's sherrif, getting a call from the bartender, came on the scene. The bear was read his rights and led off to jail.

On his way out, the bear inquired as to the charges.

"Sir, you have been arrested for trafficking in narcotics!"

"Narcotics my ass," replied the bear, "what narcotics?"

The bartender, with a little smile on his face, looked him in the eye and said, "That was a bar-bitch-you-ate!"

❦

THANKS FOR YOUR HELP, LADY!

Way over in eastern Nevada near the Utah border, a sheep herder was tending his sheep day after day, week after week, and, eventually month after month. He was becoming increasingly interested in having close bodily contact of some sort. He thought about it for many hours each day for several weeks until finally, out of desperation, he selected one of his herd to help him with his needs.

As he approached his choice of sheep, his dog...a fine border collie made a run for him with bared teeth, growling and snarling. Sheep dogs are highly protective of their charges and this one...named Harold...was not going to allow harm to come to his sheep...even from the master.

The sheepherder tried for several days to find a way to provide himself with some relief, but to no avail. Each time he tried to single out a ewe he was almost bitten. He even tried to tie Harold to some nearby sagebrush. Each time he tried, Harold would begin a disturbing howl which would lead to his breaking away and charging the man.

The herder was about to give up when in the distance he saw a figure coming toward him across the Bonneville Salt Flats. As the figure got closer, the sheepherder was, indeed, pleased to see it was a quite lovely lady, about 25 years old and magnificently built.

As she approached him and began drinking from his Bota bag, she exclaimed, "Oh, thank you sir, for saving my life. I have been wandering in the desert. My horse died about fifty miles from here and I've been on foot for two days. To show my gratitude, I will do anything for you and I mean anything!" As she said "anything," she pulled her unbuttoned shirt over her shoulders exposing her voluptuous breasts.

46

"You say you will do anything I ask?" he slyly smiled.
"Yes, anything!"
"Then why don't you start by holding that dog!"

❧

NEVER ENDING DAY

It was that same band of bad guys who fell upon the Lone Ranger in a previous story that fell upon an old prospector in the hills near the Ruby Marshes in Elko County. Remember it was the early days and people were pretty damned violent in those parts. Yes! They beat him pretty good and they stole everything he had in the world...even pulled out a gold tooth he had previously and proudly displayed. They took his blue jeans, his chambray shirt, his ratty old hat and even stripped him of his filthy underwear. Insult was going to follow injury. These bad guys took that same wet and stretched rawhide and tied this old codger's wrists to his ankles.

After kicking him many times in his bare ass, laughing and saying outrageous things about him, they climbed on their horses and headed out. It was early morning and the sun was just starting to bake him as he headed off toward where he thought Jigs, Nevada might be.

All day long he walked; bent over, naked, humiliated and getting madder by the minute. He could see a small pond up ahead where he might get a drink of water. Approaching it slowly and deliberately watching for snakes and traps that might be set close to the water, he leaned down to drink and immediately lost his balance, falling face first into a sticky algae covered mudhole. Damned near drowned! He did get his fill of water before leaving the waterhole.

47

He had to rest and finding a Pinion Pine he sat down on a not-too-hot rock, leaned against the tree and fell asleep.

When he awoke, he felt a cool breeze and realized he better get along because he didn't want to be out in the hills after dark. There were lots of animals that would eat on him. Mountain lions would love to go for him seeing that he could not defend himself. A coyote, a hungry coyote would do the same thing but take a lot longer killing him.

In the distance he could just make out a light. As he approached he could see that it was a lone cowboy sitting on a log in front of a good sized fire. He felt like he was going to be rescued from this degrading nightmare.

"Hey, stranger, I'm unarmed and I'm comin' into your camp. Hold your fire!"

He must have looked a strange-sight...walking, more like waddling, through the sagebrush, into the light of the fire. The cowboy had his hand at his gun.

As he got closer to the fire he began telling his story. "Son, it's been hell. A band of thieves stole everything I had, my burro, my grubstake, the few flakes of color I had collected in two months of diggin.' They beat me, stripped me of all my clothes, and set me off in the desert after tying me up this way. My hands are numb, my feet are bloody and swollen, I'm tired, hungry and pissed. I been wandering in the desert, the sage brush has kilt me, the sun has almost made me blind!"

It was then that the cowboy got up off his rock, looked at the naked, bent over man in front of him and as he unbuttoned his pants said, "Old timer, this sure has been your unlucky day!"

❦

YES, THERE ARE SOME THINGS
YOU DON'T TELL!

A non-descript little church on the outskirts of Carlin, Nevada, had a list of parishioners that would impress no one. Try as he might, the new minister could not create enthusiasm and thus build his fundamentalist membership. There were several options available to him. He could bring in a hot shot...someone like Jimmy Bakker, but we know what happened to Jimmy and Tammy Faye. Jimmy Swaggert was probably doing something else, and besides, there wasn't enough money to bring anyone of note into this little gold mining town some 270 miles east of Reno.

Our minister, a good man named Elvis Clearwater, had a thought. He would stimulate the congregation to get involved in the message. Yes! That had to work!

The next Wednesday night's service he began:

"Tonight we are going to get right with the Lord by confessing our sins. We are going to tell it all, tell it all, tell it all, brothers and sisters," said the preacher.

At first there was absolutely no interest in telling anything. People looked at their shoes and examined their fingernails.

"I'll tell it all, Brother Clearwater, I'll tell it all," said Sam Flint, a man of severely tarnished reputation which further contributed to a strong disposition to drinking spirited beverages. Many thought he did the imbibing all too frequently and which everyone knew he was doing this evening.

"Tell it, brother," said Elvis, encouraging Sam to help get things started.

"I've lied and stole," said Sam not too ashamedly.

"Tell it, my friend, tell it all!"

49

"I've drunk liquor, and beer, and lots of wine, and I even got drunk on brandy one time," grinned Sam.

"Tell it, brother, tell it all!"

"I've played the dice and lost the rent money!" said Sam. The crowd gasped a little, but listened intently.

"I've cheated on my old lady, and I've lusted after every good looking gal in town," Sam smiled just a little.

"Brother, tell it, tell it, tell it all!" said the Rev. Clearwater.

"I've even gone so far as to have sex with a goat!" blurted Sam to a stunned audience.

On hearing this last confession, the minister shouted, "I'm damned if I'd told that!"

❦

THE COUNTESS

Let me tell you about a lady I met in Pioche, Nevada in early 1973. She was a countess of sorts or something like that having come from the old country. She was full of stories about her former life, her present state and her plans for the few remaining years of her life. At 82 and in declining health she did not make long-range plans. However, she did buy green bananas and long novels.

The countess had a host of friends about whom she related endless stories and most of them full of intricate detail and elaboration.

Countess Hermione Goldstone was the name she was most proud of and the name she used most. She encouraged people simply to call her "Countess."

Tricksy was one of her closest friends. In her early days, Tricksy first worked in and later managed the Hot Spot Ranch (brothel), in Ely, Nevada. Ely was a little mining town about an hour north of Pioche. Copper had been discovered there and nearly every year the great gaping open pit mine kept getting bigger and bigger. Anyway, Tricksy gave up the working girl life and married one of her steady customers appropriately named John. Now John was the amorous type, thoughtful and considerate even after twelve years of marriage. He paid Tricksy much attention on a daily basis.

One day, the Countess was having some gin drinks at Tricky's home as they usually did on Thursdays. Tricksy looked out the window and saw John coming up the walk with a big bouquet of flowers. "Do you see that, Countess? That means that I will have to lie on my back all night long with my legs spread apart!"

The Countess, seating herself after her short trip to the window asked, "What's the matter, Tricksy, don't you have a vase?"

It was rumored that the countess was a royal of sorts back in her native Hungary. However, royals were more of title than either status, recompense or acknowledgment by the state. She had to leave her beloved Hungary for New York when she was but 22 years old. She also left two ex-husbands and some minor trouble with the police, but she gained a new life. From New York she managed a brief tour of the south ...Charleston and Savannah...and Texas...near Lubbock before landing down in Pioche via Las Vegas.

Pioche was and is a dusty little town in southeastern Nevada noted for little. It is surrounded completely by mountains which gives it a claustrophobic air. People seem to be happy and reasonably healthy there.

She and her husband Dave (something or other) settled in Pioche after his various schemes in Las Vegas played out.

They had just enough money and a small business to see them safely to their graves, provided they did not live more than about eight years, but who's counting.

The countess was working on a book...had been for over 30 years off and on.

She had made comment to several friends that she had writer's block, everyone knew it to be a very boring piece with no possibility of being published, and if published, no possibility of meaningful sales.

In Pioche, the Countess spent a lot of time volunteering at the Grover Dills Hospital. Frequently she was a patient. She had some very real illnesses and conditions.

The real difference between the Countess and her friend Tricksy was that the latter had always known what she was and charged smart money for that service. The Countess either gave that service away or married on a whim. She prized that service, claiming once that she "...could make a homeless man build a house!" Many of her infatuations became marriages and several of those lasted years, but on one occasion her love affair-marriage barely lasted the weekend.

When she lived in Las Vegas, shortly after her fourth husband died leaving her with a nice package of cash and an acre of land way out on the strip, the countess met up with a card player named Branch Court. Branch was from Mississippi and had served 13 months in 1966 and 1967 for what might properly be called grifting or scamming, but had gone straight in recent years and was a respected poker player in many of the nicer clubs in Las Vegas. Branch volunteered that he could be counted on to win anywhere from $75 to $1000 each and every week which attracted the Countess immediately. She lived with him in a nearby motel that had been controverted into a condo project and she wondered what he did with the money on those weeks he told her he made $1000. She never found out.

On their wedding day, they made arrangements for the most expensive, festive ceremony available at the 'Chapel of the Desert' wedding joint. This chapel was adjacent to the 'Chapel on the Strip' which was close by the 'Chapel of Love Or Whatever.' At the desert facility, Branch had arranged for the $500 special package. In those days, spending $500 *was* something special. It was primarily for the couple who came to Las Vegas, hit a pretty good sized jackpot and then hit the closest wedding spot; an impulse item.

Here's what they got.

1. A limo ride from the Chapel to the courthouse to buy a license. Limo ride back to the Chapel.

2. Use of an adjoining room in the Chapel decorated to the teeth: candles, flowers, paintings, piped-in music, the works.

3. Two bottles of Cold Duck wine (champagne $9.00 extra).

4. Reception lasting up to 30 minutes for up to 8 people. (Each additional person would cost $4.00)

5. Live organ music in the Chapel.

6. Four sprays of flowers that could be taken from the reception area to the Chapel (roses $5.00 extra).

7. Services of an ordained minister. For $10 extra, the minister would give a brief homily on marriage.

8. An on-duty photographer. Included in the package were four pictures of the bride and groom's choice. Extra pictures would be $4.00 each.

9. A 20 minute reception after the wedding with two more bottles of Cold Duck.

10. A one way limo ride to a close-by destination of the newlywed's choice.

It was fun and everyone enjoyed it.

After the wedding the two moved from the condo to a small house in North Las Vegas. The Contessa got a job in a flower shop and the two watched their marriage disintegrate. They could only live together and be happy...not be married and be happy. Go figure.

After six months of fighting, they got a quickie divorce and then became friends again and lived together for several years. Branch got a call from his friends in Mississippi and tore out after brief good-byes.

Our countess married again, this time to a business man who had fallen in love with her and multi-level marketing about the same time. She had been his first convert and subsidized, though not very well, her flower shop income with soap sales.

Their garage was full of stuff! Water filters, wash-day detergents and cleansers, air filters...the works. One day a man came out and bought everything in the garage for $75.00 and both were glad to see it go, because it reminded them of lapses in judgment. David was still convinced, however, that if one person sold five other people something...anything...for $150 and those five sold five others and those 25 sold five others...then the profits that filtered back up the chain would be great and continuous. Unfortunately, if the chain worked up to 8 levels, then those involved would have totaled nearly 2,000,000. The population of Nevada in 1970 (census) was only 488,000.

When husband number six tired of the whole thing, the two moved to Pioche to take over a small grocery store.

54

David Dinsmoor and his Countess lived behind and above the small store and made a surprisingly good living off the four slot machines and liquor sales.

It wasn't long before Dave got ill and a severe depression set upon him. The countess tried about everything she knew and had learned at the hospital to bring him out of it but nothing seemed to work for long. One day she came to him saying, "David, it looks like all the money is gone. There is no other option...I'm going to have to go to Las Vegas and sell my body." Dave pleaded with her, but could not come up with a better alternative. She spent the day with Tricksy and late that evening went to his room saying.

"I did it, Dave, yes, I hitched a ride in Clyde Sparks' plane and worked the streets of Las Vegas all day. I just got back and I have $33.75 to show for it."

"Who the hell paid you seventy-five cents?"

"All 45 of them!" she giggled proudly! And with that, they got a very good laugh. Dave's health improved, his depression ended and he lived a full five years longer before he died.

Time went by and it became time for the Countess to die. It was a beautiful church ceremony, friends and acquaintances coming from as far away as Las Vegas and Reno and even from New York.

As the people filed past the open casket of the Countess, Tricksy said in a fairly loud voice, "At last, they're together!"

She returned to her seat and the lady behind her in the line sat down beside her and whispered, "What did you mean, '...at last, they're together...' The Countess was married six times."

"I know," commented Tricksy. "I was talking about her legs!"

55

MINING SUPPLIES

'Texas' Bill Wunner was in charge of Davis Mining Company operating out of Virginia City, Nevada during the historic Comstock Load era. He was a stern man, not given to humor. The story went around VC, however, that one time a Chinaman made him laugh...maybe the only time in his adult life.

He employed scores of men eager to go down into the mines because it was steady and good-paying work. They got paid a daily wage plus bonuses for extra production. Many times the bonuses exceeded their pay and for that reason, the men had to have workers who kept them supplied with lanterns, dynamite, blasting caps and fuses, to say nothing of water and continuous emptying the numerous 'chamber' pots in each shaft.

The last man that Tex hired worked only about a month. He snapped an ankle and was carried over to Doc Hall's office for repairs. A quick recovery was in doubt, the doctor said, due to the major fact that his ankle bone was protruding thru his dirty sock.

Tex had to have a supply man that day. He sent word out the job was open and had to be filled immediately. There were three applicants within the hour. One was a woman who just had a new baby. She needed the money. It might have worked except she looked the situation over and walked away. The second applicant was so drunk he fell on the path leading up to the foreman's shack and ruptured himself real good. The third candidate was a man who had recently gotten off the boat in San Francisco straight from China...he spoke some Pidgin English, was not drunk, and wanted the job bad. Tex told him, "Listen up little man, the job is yours. I want you to provide supplies to these miners. When the men have their supplies, they are happy and when they're happy, I make more money and when I make more money, I'm happy! Do you understand? All you have to do is provide the supplies, supplies, supplies...all day long and into the night, supplies, supplies, supplies...got it?" Having said that, Tex told the men he had to go into town to send a wire to the big bosses in San Francisco. He would be back about dusk.

It was getting dark when he got back to the mine. He could hear the men working down in the shafts, but he could not see the little Chinese fellow. He yelled down in the shaft for him...no response. He looked in all the places his men would go to slack off, but no Chinaman. Finally, he was walking back up to the entrance to the mine when all of a sudden this little Asian guy jumped out from behind a big bolder and shouted, "Supplies!! Supplies!!"

BE CAREFUL WHAT YOU SAY

Rick Koolman was late leaving Virginia City where he had completed a training session with some promising fencing students. From VC High School if he hurried, he could make the opening of the fencing championship in Reno. He was to officiate one of the latter matches.

As he negotiated a severe turn to the right on the twisty, very scary road down to the Truckee Meadows, he came upon a car coming straight toward him at a high rate of speed. Both cars swerved at the last possible moment to avoid a meaningful and fatal collision. They both would have gone over an 800 foot embankment to a sudden stop at the bottom. No one ever survived that fall, though quite a few had attempted it.

In an instant, Rick saw a red Miata sports car and heard the driver, a very attractive blond yell at the top of her voice, "PIG! PIG!"

Instantaneous and reflexively, Rick shot back, "BITCH! BITCH!"

He instantly regained his composure and entered the next curve under good contol. There in the middle of that curve was a big fat pig!

❧

THE ATOMIC MARTINI

Rachel, Nevada is probably the closest 'town' to a special Nevada location called Area 51, and as such has a claim on being the world's foremost center for E.T's, UFO's, aliens of all descriptions, flying saucers, and some interesting stories about of those things just mentioned. There is this bar, restaurant, motel in Rachel called "The Little A'Le' Inn" which, through its mail-outs, advertises... "From the galaxy to Earth where it's happening... 'Home of the alien burger'... Earthlings welcome...bring your favorite friend or alien for the finest in food, drinks, lodging. Have a UFO party with your friends next to Area 51. Huge gallery of interesting photographs."

The story goes this way: one evening, a man from Las Vegas wanders into a 'A'Le' Inn' bar and starts a conversation with the bartender, a man named Ted Lokke.

"How long you been working here, friend?"

"About thirty light years, the name's Ted. What kind of business brings you to these parts?" was Ted's reply to the stranger.

"I thought I'd come up here for a spell to see what's going on in Area 51, know what I mean? What kind of drinks do you specialize in by the way?" inquired the man.

"Our house specialty is the "Atomic Martini. Want one?"

"You're gonna have to explain what an Atomic Martini is before I order one," replied the Las Vegan.

"You see, there is this place in central Nye County near a government worksite called Mercury, Nevada where they test all kinds of nuclear stuff. In the early days, they was testing the first atom bomb in Nevada and one of the workers, a young man named Bud Beatly, had the notion to strap a big bottle of Vermouth right onto that first bomb. After it exploded, there was this big party and he told everybody he had invented a new Nevada cocktail, 'The Atomic Martini.' After sayin' that he took out a martini glass, poured it full of Gin (Vodka would be OK, too) and, then sorta moved the glass around in the air real gentle-like. He figured the drink got just enough Vermouth outta the air to make it perfect. It's been that way up to this day... wanna try one?" After the stranger nodded in agreement, Ted made him the 'perfect one' and gave it to him after gently waiving it around in the smoke filled barroom air. He got paid, made change, and moved on to customers at the other end of the bar.

SPACE BAR

At the other end of the bar were three cowboys and a tired looking girl of about twenty from Gabbs, Nevada who were drifting toward Las Vegas for a long weekend and found their way to the 'Inn' for a few beers and some lie-swapping.

Ted had a favorite story he always managed to tell partly for the laughs that would surely and unfailingly come and partly for the shock effect this one story... a supposedly true one...would have on the ladies present. Most conversations stopped when he began one of his stories.

"Hey, barkeep, you got a story to tell?" said Tommy Gillam, the tallest cowboy in the threesome.

Ted finished pouring a genuine draft for one of the cowboys and began, 'Over on Highway 51 just before you get to Eureka, Nevada there is this old vacant fillin' station that ain't been used for, I guess thirty-forty years. The pumps was all shot up and busted, but the place was about the same as when Mark Gregg closed her down after the 'Goldbar Mine' closed in 1952.

"There was talk around Eureka about sightin's of space ships and unidentified flying objects for several years along this stretch of "America's loneliest highway," but nothin' much came of it. Then one night there was this huge light in the sky to the west, bringing everybody out of the three bars in town. It came swift and came down fast. The talk later was...whatever it was...a space ship, meteor, comet or whatever...landed near that fillin' station. All the cowboys who could still drive jumped in their pick-ups and tore outta town.

"Meanwhile over at the fillin' station, this silver space ship had just landed and two little aliens, I'll call them Harold

60

and Helen, got out and approached the gas pumps at the station. They looked like your typical aliens...you know... big eyes, no ears, small mouths, wise looking, one of them walked right up to one of the pumps and demanded, "Take me to your leader!"

Of course, the pump didn't say nothin.' The little feller again demanded. "We are from the planet 'Jarman 10,' you must immediately take us to your leader!"

Nothing!

"We insist that you take us to your leader this instant!" shouted Harold, now a highly frustrated little gray person.

After a moment with no response forthcoming, the two little people got back in their spaceship, lifted swiftly and vanished immediately. The heroes in their pick-ups drove up just in time to see the UFO climb to about fifty miles, hesitate and fade quickly away.

The bar people got outta their trucks, looked around for signs of something...proof you know...and finding nothin' headed straight back to town at a high rate of speed.

On the space ship, the two crewmembers were busy turning knobs and switches in efforts to reach home base on 'Jarman 10.' After some effort, home base became visible on the large TV monitor before them. Their leader ...could have been a clone of the little people on the ship...inquired as to why he was being called.

"Why are you contacting home base at this time? Were you not instructed to make a close encounter of the third kind with people on the Earth planet?"

"Yes, you are correct, most exalted commander. We have just concluded such an encounter and wish to relate our findings."

"Quickly, what are those findings?" urged the commander.

"As instructed, we approached a subject and requested, then demanded we be taken to Earth's leader." The little alien spoke clearly and distinctly.

"Then what?"

"Nothing happened high commander, absolutely nothing!" responded the no-eared dwarf.

"What do you mean...you're confusing me! Please, space scientist, tell me exactly what you saw... what the Earthling did. Your words will be recorded in Jarman 10 history for billions of your countrymen to read for thousands of years to come," directed the commander slowly and deliberately.

"That's just it, nothing was said, the Earthling just stood there with his dick in his ear!"

There was a more than usual round of laughter and applause. Then, "Hey, Ted, tell us about the 'Final Report'" shouted a friend over in the corner booth.

With that Ted took out some notes and began:

"THE FINAL REPORT"

"After signing off with the base commander on Jarman 10, our little space people began putting together their final report on their trip to Earth. They would then get into their capsules for the long sleep: long journey home." Ted continued:

"Helen, we've been circling Earth for nearly forty years and watched a lot of Earth television those years. You've kept notes. Tell me what will be the essence of your report?" inquired Harold.

"Well, Harold, according to what is shown on television, Earthlings, particularly those living in the North American portion of Earth, are totally obsessed with their bodies," Helen said, going over her notes.

Ted kept the notes close by, but he had done this shtick so often he seldom referred to them.

"Starting from the top of their ugly mal-formed bodies, according to television advertising, Earthlings need to worry about the color, texture, length, and condition of their hair. There are medications and colorings, strengtheners, and softeners and something to control dandruff, although I do not know what that is... people buy these products and spend millions, no billions of Earth dollars on them each year.

"There are products to cleanse the ears of wax build up, soothe the eyes, spray in their noses, mouthwashes, toothpastes, teeth whiteners, and a host of oral antiseptics to combat germs that flourish in humans' mouths. Eyes are the subject of attention in that they are obviously inferior to eyes on 'Jarman 10.' Earthlings eyes need to be douched and lubricated often...when Earthlings begin to age a little, the eyes are the first to experience the ravages of time. Most eyes on the planet are covered with glasses that shade them, magnify distant objects or enlarge reading material. Many vane subjects change the color of their eyes by wearing something called contact lenses. These are small discs placed directly on the delicate eyeball that, some say, makes humans more attractive to other human beings.

"The skin is a covering over the entire body that protects the internal organs and must be treated to prevent drying, wrinkling, peeling and cracking and aging. I have heard nothing humans can put on their skin has the slightest age-preventing properties. My studies indicate that the area under Earthling arms is a source of constant concern. They buy billions of dollars worth of sprays and lotions and roll-on chemicals to prevent odor from offending themselves and others.

"Their faces must have this mal-odor also, for men buy colognes and after sprays to splash on themselves after they razor off little hairs growing every day there. Some males of the species have lots of hair on their faces, bodies, under their arms, mid regions and legs. While others have forces internally that prevent hair from growing on their heads and on their chests. Billions of Earth dollars are spent yearly on hair restoratives for men and hair preventatives for women. Must be painful for women to have lots of hair and some men to have none in socially important places.

"There is one body region prized above all others. It is the inguinal region, the mid region, the private parts, the sex parts, the propagation regions, the lust areas, the unmentionables, the south-of-the-border zones, yes...as some human called them..."The areas nice people don't talk about!" These areas must be just awful!

"Advertiser feel free to talk about women and the alleged problems created by "unfresh areas" of their bodies, and the wide variety of sprays and douchables available to them. It is not acceptable on TV or any other place on the planet for two men to talk about their private parts not being fresh. Men would not stand for it, women stand for it without so much as a minor protest. It has always been a wonder to me why females on Earth allow such degradation. They allow TV advertisers to dramatize 'Light Days' (something to do with their reproductive systems), 'maxi-protection,' feminine hygiene sprays, hemorrhoids, rectal itching, intestinal gases and bloating, and 'vaginal moisturizers.' If their planet partners, men, talked about their unique problems on TV, they would be called things like 'Gross, tasteless and crude!'

There is a double standard here I have concluded. "Feet are another source of advertisers' attacks. We have seen pictures of men's feet emitting foul odors, burning...actually on fire...feet being assaulted by evil looking fungus creatures, toenails growing inwardly, and generally becoming a smelly, oozing unsightly mess! Humans know feet can be a problem occasionally, but not to advertisers' extremes.

"I have heard Earthlings lament that their bodies have not evolved into the perfect forms they will become, but they are not nearly as bad as TV advertisers have depicted them! They could stop these untoward TV attacks if they wanted to.

"In several other canisters of data our little "gray people" sent back to 'Zarman 10' over the last ten to twenty Earth years were reports on certain quirks Earthlings possessed. The lists were detailed and curious.

Report #2875
"Earthlings like to fight with each other, many times to the death. They also claim their creator...sometimes called God, but also by many other names...is definitely on their side. 'Shape shifting aliens' as we are called by Earthlings, have trouble understanding how one 'God' can be on all sides, thus we dispatch such concepts as illogical.

"There are thousands of animal species on Earth...they share several ways of creating their progeny. Some animals, such as certain worm-like creatures possess both male and female reproductive mechanisms. There is no need for a sex mate. All the other animals and human beings have to 'mate' to procreate, that is, a female has to be at least in the vicinity of a male, she doesn't have to physically do anything with him...many species of fish, for example lay their eggs and leave...the male finishes the job with his fertilizer. This appears to be an inefficient and enjoyment-lacking way of species continuation.

"Female sea turtles, after physical contact with the male of that species buries her fertilized eggs in the sand; she never comes in contact with those eggs or her offspring again. Many male animals including humans 'mate' with their female counterparts for nothing more than recreational purposes and, if conception occurs, never have anything more to do with offspring creatures. Others 'mate' for life...some 'mate' for death as in the case of the lowly black spider who is entirely consumed by his sex object. The female creates her own 'widowed' condition.

"Human beings as they are called, the self-proclaimed end point of evolution on this planet, have many 'pairing off' rituals. Most go through some form of ceremony that acknowledges their commitment, take up residence and live their complete lives together. When offspring are created from this union both take care of them...about two thirds of these 'marriages' are eventually dissolved...many times with great acrimony and strong language. Then there is but one Earthling to take care of the offspring. Usually other Earthlings come along...many times very quickly...to join up with those thus separated. It is rare when those unions last for very long either.

"Some of the things that cause Earthling pairs to separate are truthful answers by the male to questions asked by the female such as:

"Do I look fat?"

"Do you think she is prettier than me?"

"If I died, would you remarry?"

"Evidently this is some sort of trap only the most skilled

males can avoid falling into. This avoidance mechanism usually takes the form of running.

"There is substantial agreement among males we have observed in the Reno, Nevada area that they have the better of life on the planet because:

They can go to the bathroom without a support group.

Dry-cleaning and haircuts are less expensive

Bathroom lines are 80 percent shorter.

A five day vacation requires only one suitcase.

They can be showered and ready to go anyplace in ten minutes.

Flowers fix everything.

They can take their shirts off on a hot day.

"In our travels, Harold and I have witnessed animosity between males and females in the workplace. For example, we have observed a female supervisor writing up a work evaluation of a male subordinate under 'personal attributes' she had a list of negative comments:

"I would not allow this employee to breed. Men he supervises would follow him anywhere, but only out of morbid curiosity. He sets low personal standards, then consistently fails to achieve them. This employee is depriving a village somewhere of an idiot! He has the knack of making strangers immediately. He brings a lot of joy just by leaving a room. When his intelligence quotient reaches 50, he should sell. If you see two men talking and one looks bored, he is the other man. He's been working with glue too much. This employee should go far...and soon, I hope."

"It was learned these two earlier had a temporary 'pairing

off' ending in the copious use of bad language, threats and subsequent termination of employment.

"We observed, in the Hawthorn area, we think, a little female about six Earth years of age asking her father, "Daddy, what is sex?"

The father took the next several minutes to explain about reproduction, genitals, eggs, sperm, intercourse, gestation, birthing and took pride in doing a brief but thorough job of explaining the birds and the bees phenomenon. The little girl looked shocked and dismayed so the father asked, "Why did you want to know about sex right now?"

"Oh, mommy said lunch would be ready in a couple of secs..."

"Many males of the human species, having experienced numerous encounters with females of their same age or younger, have dedicated their lives to mating only older women. Reasons they give for doing this are numerous also.

"An older woman will never wake the male up in the middle of the night and ask, "What are you thinking?" An older woman doesn't care what the male thinks. And older woman is a cheaper date. A younger woman will cost the male 12 beers, but an older woman will mate after a cup of herbal tea.

"Older women can run faster because they always wear sensible shoes. And older women will never accuse a younger male of 'using her' because she is using him!

"An older woman will never accuse the male of 'stealing the best years of her life' because chances are, someone else has already stolen them.

❧

"An eighty year old male was observed at a doctor's office in Carson City proudly exclaiming that his new wife, an eighteen year old girl was going to have a baby. The doctor thought for a moment and replied, 'Let me tell you a story. I knew a man who was a frequent hunter. He never missed an opportunity to go hunting. One day he went out in a bit of a hurry and accidentally grabbed his umbrella instead of his shot gun.

"So he is in the woods out by Topaz Lake and suddenly a gigantic bear jumped up in front of him! He raised his umbrella, pointed it at the bear and squeezed the handle.

"Mr. Jones, do you know what happened?" the doctor asked.

Dumfounded, the old man replied, "No, I don't!"

The doctor continued. "The bear dropped dead right there in front of him!"

"That's impossible!" shouted the old man in disbelief! "Someone else must have shot that bear!"

The doctor replied with a little grin, "That's kind what I'm getting at!"

❧

"After all the canisters were filled with similar observations gleaned over nearly half an Earth century Harold and Helen got into their cryogenic capsules for the journey back to their home on "Zarman 10."

The spaceship zoomed away from Earth leaving behind thousands of sightings by Earthlings and equal number of denials by governments."

Ted collected his applause and tips and took his break. He went over to a booth where some buddies were slamming beers and asked for an update on UFO sightings.

"Ain't seen one lately, Ted, but I heard a space ship landed on the Vegas strip. Yeh! The aliens got propositioned within 2 minutes of landing and were handed a booklet containing $50 in coupons and were mugged before they could get back on board!—true story!" said Ted's friend.

"Yeh, right—true story," replied Ted.

❦

PILOT LIGHTS

"I don't think I like being a test pilot anymore!" exclaimed Chet Pinkley. "I've been doing it so long I'm not as scared as I used to be or should be. It's not exactly like driving a brand new Buick around a test track to see if all systems function. When I get in a new plane, that ship has never left the ground. Oh, sure, it has been checked out on paper...theoretically it is safe as a city bus, but you don't drive a bus at 50,000 feet."

Chet and his buddy, Wayne, were just about at the end of a twenty year career checking out new aircraft for a host of builders. They both got assigned to "Groom Lake," an airfield in a desolate, remote part of Nevada generally called "Area 51" to test out a new experimental craft being developed by the Air Force. This plane was a black, sleek fighter craft which rumor says was not supposed to be detectable on radar. In addition there were several systems that had never been installed on military aircraft. These desperately needed "empirical testing." Both he and Wayne were called in for this.

Each pilot was separately and repeatedly sworn to secrecy and had been given the "top" designation; neither had the least interest in telling their business to anyone. That was a chief determinant in their being repeatedly called in on sensitive assignments.

One night Chet and Wayne were having drinks in their base quarters and, knowing they were not scheduled to fly for several days, both had one or two too many drinks. They laughed about "too many" drinks, each asking, "Too many for what?" The next day would be filled with the same stuff today and yesterday were filled with...not much!

"Chet, what was the most terrifying flight experience you ever had?" asked a toasted Wayne.

"That's easy, Wayne. I was flying over north Africa on a reconnaissance assignment when my equipment indicated missiles had been launched against me, probably by Col. Khadafi. They had me pretty well locked in and I began my textbook evasion maneuvers. At first they seemed to work, but then I realized those things were closing and fast. Were they heat seeking missiles? I didn't know then but I know now. I kept swerving and climbing and twisting and doing cartwheels and somersaults, but they kept getting closer. So here's what happened. I reached in my survival back pack and grabbed two flares, opened my canopy enough to pitch out the lit flares, killed my engines and did a hard left. I saw the missiles head right for the flares and explode! The shock wave was awesome! By God, I shit myself!" exclaimed the pilot, jumping to his feet!

"That's understandable, Chet, you were excited, you narrowly escaped death, your adrenaline was pumping! Sure, that's understandable how that happened!" consoled Wayne.

"Not over north Africa, Wayne, JUST NOW!"

The two got a very good laugh out of that one. They had just enough hooch to make that unbelievable story somewhat believable. They had another drink, saluting the story and the telling of it.

"Chet you had me believing you there for a moment. I'm going to tell you a true story, however. I was on this assignment to test a new parachute for the navy. After I was instructed in the packing of the damned thing, they took me to 20,000 feet and I jumped without fear. It was only about my 750th jump...nothing new for me. At ten thousand, I picked out the spot in the desert where the trucks were waiting...down near a trailer park. At 7500 I pulled the ripcord. Well, Chet, nothing happened! I remembered the product manual and mentally thumbed through the parts about 'If 'X' doesn't happen then do 'Y'!' The next thing to do on the list was to grab the ripcord with both hands and give three quick tugs. Still nothing! Panic was just about to set in! From below me, at that same instant, I saw something, looked like a man coming straight at me from below. It was a man, all blackened and sporting a look of utter terror!

"Hey, man," I shouted, "Do you know how to operate a parachute?"

The man looked me squarely in the eye as we passed at about ten feet and shouted, "Man, I don't even know how to light the gas stove in my trailer!"

Both men totally enjoyed their evening together. The next three weeks—all at night—they tested the new aircraft over

72

the southeastern portion of Nevada. Not unexpectedly, there were something like sixty three reports of flying saucers from as far away as Tonopah and Hawthorn.

ॐ

SPACE ALIEN ATTACKS LOCAL RESIDENTS NEAR MT. WHEELER

Two Ely residents hiking in the foothills of Mt. Wheeler on Thursday reported sighting an alien spaceship. They were chased, the story goes, by a huge nine foot tall creature as "Fast as hell!" J. Kendal Rirey, 62, an Ely physician and Bruce Christensen, 39, another local physician both related similar stories though they were separated in their hurry to put distance between themselves and the alleged "monster."

"We were hiking along and both of us saw this spaceship circle over us and land without a sound. The doors opened and this gigantic creature came running out," reported Dr. Rirey. "He made straight for us and I could hear his big feet breaking up the sagebrush down in the draw!"

When asked what the two men did next, Dr. Christensen calmly reported that he sat down on a big rock and began putting on the jogging shoes he brought with him in his backpack.

"You're not going to try to outrun that thing coming at us at 25 to 30 miles an hour are you, Bruce?" asked a truly astonished J. Kendal.

Dr. Christensen was reported to have said, "No, J.K., all I have to do is outrun you!"

Both men escaped to tell their tales!

Nevada Light Blue Humor

LAS VEGAS...ONCE CALLED "THE MEADOWS"

LAS VEGAS...ONCE CALLED "THE MEADOWS"

In the early seventies when I first came to Nevada, Las Vegas was coming into its own. It had outstripped Reno as the largest city in the state in the 1970 census and was steadily gaining power in the state legislature. People in Reno were beginning to get the idea that Las Vegas would be the 'power' and there was nothing to be done about it.

Natives of Las Vegas—and trust me, there are few natives—at that time were a haughty bunch. They insisted, much like San Franciscans insisted, the name of their city not be violated. There was a small bunch of people who would correct you were you to say "Vegas." As the town grew, they learned maybe they should redirect their energies and the name "Vegas" took off. Remember the TV show called "Vega$?" The show depicted our city as a violent, mob ridden, corrupt, women debasing, evil empire. The show was terrible, but it lasted several seasons and possibly did a measure of damage to some residents' egos.

The term Las Vegas, in Spanish, means "the meadows." Were my life and eternal soul to depend on it, I could not picture that portion of abject desert ever being a meadow! Yet, I've talked with life long residents of that city who tell me, at one time, you could not even have basements any where in the valley because of the high water table. Agonizingly hard to believe!

Many people in the north refer to that southern city as "Lost Wages," forgetting about all the wages lost in clubs in Reno and other northern towns. Most Renoites don't give one little damn about Las Vegas. Never did, never will! And, of course, vice versa...in spades!

The state of Arizona says it has old maps and documents that show Las Vegas is actually in Arizona. This thought has brought tears to the eyes of many northern Nevadans. The thought that they could lose Las Vegas to another state has frightened and saddened them. Others feel that a line should be drawn eastward from San Luis Obispo, California, through the big valley, through the Sierra, south of Tonopah over to the Utah border. The southern portion consisting of Las Vegas environs would then annex to the southern portion of California...forming one very homogenious 'South California.' Reno and the rest of northern Nevada could join with San Francisco, etc., to form 'North California.' This would be much like North and South Dakota, Virginia and West (by God) Virginia. Well, that ain't gonna happen, but it's a thought, besides, people in Reno don't want much to do with those northern Californians either.

Las Vegas just gets bigger and bigger with no end in sight. They make millions imploding those old casinos, and building new ones, they make millions entertaining an international clientele, they make millions, lodging, wining and dining millions. Each year their gaming winning percentages increase dramatically and five thousand people move there each month.

Is the mob still active in Las Vegas? Don't ask! Nevadans are told that we have the strongest gaming control board in the world...that other states new to legalized gaming look to Nevada as their model for legitimacy. Does that mean

there is absolutely no hanky-panky going on? No, it probably
doesn't mean that.

Let's talk about some of the humorous stuff that goes on
in Vegas, Las Vegas.

LAS VEGAS

Las Vegas, right there in the hot desert.
Started there to fulfill a dream
By a crazy man who had an eye for
The fast lane, who later would be shot
In the eye for that dream.

Las Vegas in the seventh largest state
Maybe driest, maybe hottest
And maybe the most liberal and yet
Most conservative at the same time.
Most practical as well?

Las Vegas, the most fun place to visit
All throughout the last half of the
Twentieth century...ya wanna bet!
The world's entertainment capital.
Buildings scraping the skies!

Argeepee

TAKE A SEAT, PLEASE!

Sam Boyd Stadium, the home of the University of Nevada, Las Vegas, Runnin' Rebels (Go Big Red!) was about as full as it gets...that is, about one half full...and the game between the Rebels and the Wolfpack of the University of Nevada, Reno, was well into the first quarter. The two teams were interstate rivals and UNLV had just recently hired away head football coach, Jeff Horton from the Wolfpack. Mr. Horton would soon leave UNLV after a dismal won/loss record. This promised to be a hard fought, grudge-type contest, however.

It wasn't the Running Rebels year and already the Pack was two touchdown ahead when this UNLV freshman student headed up the steps looking for his seat. His arms were full of 1) two hot dogs; 2) a Pepsi; 3) peanuts; 4) popcorn; 5) football program; 6) binoculars; and 7) a small radio.

He located his row and commenced annoying about thirty people on his way to his seat which was almost in the center of the section. People had to stand up to let him pass and, on at least two occasions, catch him to prevent his toppling over. He got to his seat and caused this huge man to shift over...also this small woman had to move to let him sit.

No sooner had he seated himself than from out of the crowd somewhere above him came the clear and very distinctive yell, "Hey, Steve!!!"

On hearing this, our UNLV student stood up, his arms still full of stuff, turned around and looked over the sea of fans. He could see no one waiving back or standing up or anything and at that moment he lost his balance and fell over the fat man seated next to him.

It took more than two minutes for this embarrassed young man to collect his belongings, wipe the Pepsi off the not-too-pleased big buy and return to the seated position. Then it happened again, "Hey, Steeeeeve!" implored the enthusiastic voice.

Seeing that his neighbor was about to get up again, the fat man offered to take his stuff to avoid wearing it again. The student thanked him and turned to locate the source of the greeting. No one waived, no one greeted, no one did anything.

The student retrieved his refreshments and gear from his highly annoyed neighbor and returned to watch the game.

This time the voice had become impatient, "Hey, Steeeeve!!"

And with that the freshman stood up, turned around so sharply that he emptied his cup of soda on the lady sitting next to him and yelled back, "Dammit, My name is not Steve!"

RELATED

A sunny day in Las Vegas...what else...the sun shines 92% of the time. Anyway, it was a hot, dry day and these two guys are standing at a bus stop on the west end of the strip. One of the guys asks:

"Hey, Bro, where you from?"

"I'm from South Carolina, Jack, where you from?"

"No lie, I'm from South Carolina. What city you from?"

"I'm from Charleston, how 'bout you?"

"Man, I'm from Charleston, too! What part of Charleston?

"Spring Street," replied the man.

"Spring street? What address on Spring Street?"

"Corner Spring and Wentworth, number 369, upstairs in the back."

"Boy, what yo' woman name?"

"My woman name be Carmella, why you ax?"

"Put 'er there, brother, we is husbands-in-law!"

YOU CAN'T WIN!

It was Arthur Fiedler and the Boston Pops at their very best. They were performing at the Thomas and Mack arena in Las Vegas...it may have been Arthur's last big event before retiring.

He had just finished a medley of tunes by Gershwin and was about to begin an extended foray into Wagner and that famous "Ride of the Valkyries" when a shrill voice came from the back of the audience.

"Hey, Arthur, play *Melancholy Baby!*"

Well, Arthur ignored the man, and showing a little annoyance, began the Wagner piece. At the end he collected his applause and as he was about to lapse into a "Carousel" selection, he heard: "Hey, Arthur, play *Melancholy Baby!*" This time the heckler was showing a little impatience.

Undaunted, but further annoyed, the great maestro directed a beautiful and full rendition of *If I Loved You.*

At the end, yes, again, "Hey Arthur, why don't you play *Melancholy Baby?*"

The script called for a thundering *Beethoven's Fifth Symphony* replete with a crescendo of kettle drums and clashing cymbals. During the build up, Arthur mentally said,

"Why the hell not, if the Boston Pops isn't flexible, then we are nothing...I'll do it as soon as I finish."

As the audience settled down from the Fifth, Arthur gave notice that the orchestra would go directly to *"Melancholy Baby."*—Applause!

And play it they did! It was outstanding!

When the piece was winding down, Arthur mused he would grant a brief moment for the heckler to thank him or give a couple of "Bravos."

It was over...thunderous applause, there was a pause, then the silver haired director heard:

"Hey, Arthur! Show us your dick!"

CREATIVE WRITING

Once on an airplane going to Las Vegas to interview for several jobs, I checked out the airline magazine...you know, the ones that occasionally have interesting photographs about uninteresting subjects and provocatively titled articles about non-current events. There in the back of the magazine were these advertisements from several "universities" offering diplomas and degrees by simply providing some "life experience" data and mailing in some fees. I thought it would be fun to create a new resume for the Las Vegas positions being sought. I banged away on my lap top and came up with the following gem:

Richard Gamble, B.S., M.S., JD, Ph.D., MD.
55512 Won Too Street
Las Vegas, Nevada 89000

Career goals: after extensive and expensive college and university enrollment and graduation, it is my goal to use the advance degrees accumulated to increase the visibility, productivity and economic picture of my employer.

Education: was educated in public schools in Gabbs, Nevada. After which enrolled in Pacific-Atlantic-Western University located in Kona, Hawaii in September, 1974. Received bachelor's diploma in business administration later that month.

Enrolled in the "Master of Science" program at the famous Hercules-Summit University in El Segundo, CA. in October, 1974, receiving my diploma in early November 1974.

Was accepted in the "Doctor of Jurisprudence" program at renowned Latouche University, Hushpuckinah, MS. in November 1974, receiving my law diploma (with high honors) in early December, 1974.

In early January, 1975, was enrolled in the prestigious "Millennium University" located in Albuquerque, NM., was presented the prized "Doctorate in Business Administration" diploma in late January, 1975.

Returned to my Alma Mater...Pacific-Atlantic-Western University and received my "Doctor of Medicine" diploma in February, 1975.

References on request.

SIT DOWN, STAND UP

Las Vegas stand up comedy—the very best in the country, may be accompanied by a drummer skilled at rim shots...it's effective, but not necessary.

"Evening ladies and gentlemen, my name is Vinnie Torino and I'll be your host for tonight's comedy show. Our first entertainer has just completed an extended engagement at the Motel Six in downtown Parump, Nevada. Please give a big Las Vegas welcome to Phil Mundo.

"Hi, folks, I'm Glad to be here after those audiences in Parump. Boy are they vicious...last night a senior citizen sat there the whole act sharpening her knitting needle. But I'm glad to be here...Las Vegas audiences are the best in the world.

"I'm glad the economy is doing so well. Things, however, were pretty grim for the mafia last year; yeh, they had to lay off four judges. Last winter it was so cold I saw a lawyer with his hands in his own pockets. I just read about two gay Las Vegas judges who tried each other!

"Those lawyers, huh? Remember the case where the kid shot his mom and dad? His lawyer threw him on the mercy of the court as being an orphan!

"Yeh, that other case where the bum was smoking in bed and burned the flop house down...at his trial, his lawyer addressed the jury. '...And I intend to prove, ladies and gentlemen of the jury, that bed was on fire when my client got into it!'

"Ah yes, golf...that's the game where a guy chases a ball all over the county when he's too old to chase women.

"Two guys were in the locker room at the Desert Inn Country Club changing clothes after a round of golf. One guy started putting on a bra. 'What are you doing, Harry? How long have you been wearing that thing?' asked his friend? 'I've been wearing it ever since my wife found it in the pocket of my sports coat."

"I checked in at that New Mirage Hotel last night and

immediately had to call the manager and complain. I said, 'All right, who's the comedian who left the plunger in the toilet?' —ouch!

"My friend Bill has been seeing a hooker who works at the whore house sixty miles north of Vegas. She came home with a baby last week...said the baby was a real brothel sprout!

"What do you think? If all the bones buried in those shallow graves in the desert outside Las Vegas started glowing, do you think we could save on our electric bills?"

"In a recent monologue by Jay Leno on 'The Tonight Show' he said he'd read that Las Vegas would run out of water by year 2007. Then he said, 'So what, Las Vegas ran out of taste in 1952!'

"When a reporter from the *Review Journal* asked the mayor and the city council what they thought about the comment by Jay Leno that Las Vegas had no taste, they all shouted, 'What's this 'no taste' shit?'

"My friend Bill, I just told you about, is really dumb. He thinks a mouse pad is a condo for high class mice. Yeh, Bill is convinced a sectional sofa is designed for an occasional piece. Bill is so simple he thinks 'cremation' is something you put in your coffee and he just knows the term 'bronchial' refers to that football team in Denver. Boy is he dumb!

"I'm telling you, Bill ain't real smart, just the other day he was asked to become a Jehovah's Witness, but he declined because he said he didn't see the accident. He said his idea of a perfect woman was one who makes love for five straight hours then turns into a Pastrami sandwich and a six pack!

"Boy was I starved this afternoon. I went to this pizza place on Paradise Avenue and ordered the biggest pizza in the place. The guy behind the counter asked me if I wanted it cut in six or eight slices and I quickly told him I wanted eight slices 'cause I was really hungry!

"I'm dating this beautiful blond gal from Searchlight, Nevada. Boy is she a honey! She said she had recently divorced and I asked her if she could remember her wedding vows...she said, 'You betcha...A,E,I,O, U!'

"She told me she was riding down the road and saw this blond-headed lady rowing away in a small boat out in an Alfalfa field. She said she pulled her car over and went to the edge of the field and said, "Hey, you're giving blondes a bad name out there in a rowboat in the middle of an alfalfa field. We're trying to shake the image of blondes being dumb, of being stupid. You really are making me mad, in fact, if I could swim, I'd be out there kicking your ass!

"How about all this construction on the strip? I heard the architectural firm used for the overall design was composed of two hookers and a pit boss.

"I went to my mechanic last week and told him my Jaguar wasn't getting much gas mileage. He told me to do like all other Jag owners do. I asked him what that was and he said, 'Lie about it!'

"During the mid east oil crisis not long ago, I did my part, yeh...I put a brick in the gas tank of my Jag and I also turned the thermostat back to 68 degrees.

"My wife and my daughter were at the San Diego Zoo. When they got to the Lion's area, my curious daughter asked her mom, 'How do lion's make love?' My wife replied, 'I don't know, your daddy is a Kiwanian!'

"I've started reading, yeh, I don't have much time so I'm reading short books. Here's a few I've just finished. *A Journey Through the Mind of Dan Quayle*; *Saddam Hussein's Tips on World Dominance*; *Mike Tyson's Guide to Dating*

Etiquett; Bob Dole, the Wild Years, and the shortest one yet, *How I Made a Million Dollars in multi-level marketing!*

"I went home the other night and started packing. My wife asked me what I was doing and I told her I was going to Australia. 'Yeh, there's five women for every man. I'm going there to make a fortune selling myself. I can make $50 every time I make one of those ladies happy!" She started packing, too, and I asked her where she was going. 'I'm going to Australia, too, I wanna see how you live on $50 a month!'

"I saw a car the other day with two bumper stickers I hadn't seen before. One read *'I Heart My Dog Head'*...and the other read *'Where Am I Going And Why Am I In This Hand Basket?'*

"Those lawyers, huh...can't live without 'em! Did you hear about the word processor my lawyer just bought? No matter what font you pick, everything comes out in fine print.

"Let's not leave lawyers...my favorite subject...until I tell you the difference between a porcupine and two lawyers in a Porsche. With the porcupine, the pricks are on the outside!

"What do you buy a graduate from law school? A lobotomy!

"What's the difference between a lawyer and a herd of buffalo? The lawyer charges more!

"Did you hear about the terrorist who hijacked a plane full of lawyers going to Reno for the Nevada Bar Association Annual Convention? He threatened to release one each hour if his demands weren't met.

"How about that new sushi bar over on Sahara owned by a law firm. Nice name too...Sosumi!

"Where can you find a good lawyer in Vegas? Out in the desert in a shallow grave.

"This Vegas judge called the two lawyers on the case

before him into his chamber and said, 'Attorney Cheatum, you gave me $15,000 to fix this case and Attorney Fleece, you gave me $10,000 to do the same thing. Cheatum, here's $5,000 back, now we'll try this case on its merits!'

"Land is so expensive in Las Vegas they have to bury two men in the same grave. Yeh, the other day at the cemetery, I saw a tombstone that read 'Here lies a Las Vegas lawyer and an honest man.'

"I just heard about Ted Kosinski's lawyer. Seems he was looking around the cabin Ted used to live in and came across an unopened letter. When he opened it, the bomb blew his left arm and left leg completely off. It's OK...he's All Right now!

"A drunk lawyer staggers out on the ice to do some fishing. He hears a loud, booming voice saying, 'You will find no fish under this ice!' The drunk asks, 'How do you know that, are you God?' 'No, I'm the manager of this hockey rink!'

"Isn't that Las Vegas Sundown Hospital something? They've started a new transplant program, but I don't think it will bring in a lot of money, after all how many people want to transplant warts, hemorrhoids, and zits?

"There's this dentist over on Paradise who has become a real scientist. Yeh, he has developed a technique to take the green off your teeth and the green out of your wallet at the same time!

"My wife got back from a visit to her doctor and told me, 'He gave me the best breast exam!' I said, 'Charlotte, for God's sake, he's a dentist!'

"My wife, you know, works in a doctor's office. The other day she went into an examining room and caught her doctor having sex with one of his patients. 'Doctor, how could you,' she asked in a very shocked tone. He responded, 'Relax, every doctor sooner or later has sex with his patients!' 'But you're a veterinarian! Thanks, folks, you've been a great audience!"

"Let's hear it for Phil Mundo...Phil may be back later on, it all depends on whether or not Phil gets lucky backstage."

❦

INSULTS ABOUND!

Danny Winters and his wife Helen were having their 40th wedding anniversary and were in Las Vegas at the Flamingo Hilton Hotel...the very place they celebrated their wedding. They checked in late on a Friday afternoon and just had time to dress and go to the Stratosphere Restaurant for their 7:30 dinner reservation.

Danny asked Helen to go on up to the room and get started. He would go by the bar and have a drink before joining her.

He entered the bar and seated himself, ordered his favorite drink...VO and water...and as he was sipping it, a very attractive young lady sat down beside him and they began to talk. Danny quickly determined that she was a prostitute and he thought he would have a little fun with her.

"I'll give you five dollars for your services," he whispered.

In a low, but very direct response, she told him what he could do with each of those five one dollar bills and left the scene.

Danny went up to his room, dressed and with Helen by his side walked through the huge casino area toward the cab stand.

Just then, this very attractive looking girl he had met earlier in the bar came up to him and said, "See what you get for five dollars?"

❧

HANG UPS

Helen, not understanding the comment, shrugged it off and the two went to the Stratosphere and had a wonderful meal and returned to the Hilton to watch a little TV, then prepare for bed.

Helen took over the bathroom first and took an inordinately long time to get ready for bed. When she came out, she quickly got into bed. Danny then went in...it was his turn.

While Danny was showering and brushing up, Helen thought it might be a good idea, since they would be reenacting their wedding night activities, she needed to limber up a little.

A few push ups on the bed and some arm swings plus five deep knee bends should do it she thought. She then got in bed and began a few leg lifts over her head. After the third lift, her feet got caught in the fabric of the big headboard of the double bed. She tried to free herself before her husband came back, but that just didn't happen. There she was, on her back, naked, with both legs over her head caught in the headboard. Quite a picture!

Just then Danny came out of the bathroom putting on his glasses that were fogged over due to the hot shower. He took one look at his wife of 40 years laying in bed and said, "Helen, for God's sake, comb your hair and put your teeth

91

back in, you look more like your mother every day!"

TEA TIME

It was called the Mission of Mercy. It was located about 65 miles due north of what is now Las Vegas in an area that is now the Nevada test site. It was sagebrush, Joshua trees, and not much else, save desert, turtles and snakes!

The mission was staffed by a priest, a mother superior and four nuns in various stages of their training. The old adobe chapel had been built by early believers and the purpose of the mission was to provide some level of salvation to the few Indians, Mexicans and drifters who wandered through the Nevada territory during that period.

The Father had spent time in Australia and had fallen in love with it. He had brought to this new assignment in America three small Koala bears that acted as constant and pleasant reminders of his past life down under. They were his house pets and companions and pretty much had the run of the place.

One of the Father's quirks was each day he would brush his koalas and collect this fur until he had enough to boil down a fine tea. It served as one of his amusements and satisfied his pets, but also, as he attested to the nuns in his charge, this tea had medicinal properties he was certain.

One day there was this banging on the gate and as the nuns proceeded to open it, they came face to face with a man who looked as if he had experienced many hard times...most of them very recently. He introduced himself to the Sisters as Jason Martin who was on his way to find gold in the western foothills of the Sierra Mountains. His uncle had written telling him all about striking it rich by just swooshing some rocks and dirt around in a fry pan and picking out the nuggets. On his way west he had gotten lost and had been wandering around in this severe desert for several days. He asked for some water, food and a place to stay for the night. What he wanted most, however, was directions on how to get out of the desert and over the mountains to the promised land.

After he had washed up and rested a spell, it was time for dinner. The Sisters had prepared a meal of lamb stew, beans, bread and tea. The father introduced Mr. Martin to his unusual tea.

After dinner and endless praying, the man had thoughts of retiring. He asked the priest, "Father, that is the most unusual tea I've tasted. What exactly is it?"

"My son," replied the Father, "this tea is made from the fur of that magnificent animal from Australia named the Koala Bear. I have three of them here and I will be glad to let you see them tonight or tomorrow morning before you depart. They are the pride of the Mission of Mercy!"

"In the morning will be fine, Father, but let me ask you one question about the tea. Do you use a filter? The reason I ask this question is that I seem to have a mouthful of tiny hairs as we speak."

The priest bristled somewhat and replied, "My son, The Koala Tea Of Mercy Is Unstrained!"

CHAPTER AND VERSE

Ron Hackett was walking down the strip one day when a very dishelveled man approached him and made a very strong appeal for a few dollars. He said his job as an architect had been abolished, his severance pay had long since run out, his creditors were calling...and his job search had turned up nothing...save multi-level marketing.

Ron looked him over, slipped him a ten spot and gave him some strong advice.

"Sir, I think you would be well-advised if you would make an appointment to see your minister for some counseling." Ron was thanked profusely and the man went on his way.

Two weeks later, Ron was at his Las Vegas Kiwanis club meeting and saw this same man seated near the speaker's table. As he approached the man, he noticed this time he was quite handsomely attired, shoes shined, hair cut and he looked very presentable.

"Good day, sir, aren't you the man I met on Las Vegas Boulevard who I helped with a little cash and advice?"

"Yes sir, and for that I am thankful. Your financial assistance and direction for me to see my minister helped me back on my feet. I'm back and I intend to join this service club as soon as I can."

"That is a success story if I ever heard one," replied Ron. "What is it the minister said or did to turn your life around?"

"He simply directed me to a certain chapter in the good book," said the man.

"What chapter is that?" asked Ron, hoping to gain some valuable insights.

"Chapter 11," commented the man with a smile.

❦

FOOD FOR THOUGHT

Before meeting Ron Hackett in the previous story, this same, nicely dressed, though somewhat disheveled middle aged man approached a passerby on the Las Vegas strip and related to him the following story. "Sir, if I could have but a word with you. My name is William Space and I am from Clinton, South Carolina. One night not long ago I had a dream showing me that if I were to sell my modest home and travel to Las Vegas, I could assuredly win my fortune on the mega-bucks slot machine. Well, sir, my family and I have been here for almost 10 days and I have unfortunately not won the jackpot. My wife and family have not eaten in almost two days and I implore you, sir, to help us out!"

This kind Las Vegan was touched by this sad story and was obliged to help. He asked skeptically. "Sir, I'll help you, but how can I be sure that if I do give you some money, you won't waste it on gambling?"

"Rest assured, sir, that whatever money you give me will go toward buying *food* for my family...gambling money, I got!"

❦

FAMILIAR TOOLS

A story went around the Las Vegas medical community in the mid seventies about an insurance company having to settle an unusual and humorous case.

The Harkermans and the Jeffreys were neighbors and the

two husbands were always outside working on their cars. One day Betty Harkerman looked out the window and saw only the legs of a very dirty pair of coveralls sticking out from under her husband's car. She called, "Harry, soups on! Why don't you stop where you are, clean up and let's eat?"

In a few minutes, she realized Harry didn't hear her over the din of the hammering he was doing. Betty went outside to deliver the message anew. She approached the jacked-up sports car and, looking down, saw that her husband's fly was open. Giving into what she later called in impish impulse, she bent down and gave his exposed genitalia a wholesome tickle.

What happened next went something like this: a reflex action took over and the mechanic's head began bumping up and down until he was quite unconscious. About then, her husband appeared, the shocked Mrs. Harkerman demanded an answer to her question, "Where in the hell did you come from?

"What's going on? I just stepped over to grab one of Bill's tools," replied Harry.

"I'm afraid I did, too," Betty said.

Since Bill was still knocked out, Betty called the paramedics who came very quickly, they checked him out and, after consulting with the trauma center, were instructed to bring him in. As poor Bill was being taken to the ambulance, Betty told the crew what happened. The paramedics got so tickled they broke up with laughter, and in that process, dropped the stretcher. Bill suffered a broken leg and subsequently sued the ambulance company.

❦

ASK THE RIGHT QUESTIONS

Two Las Vegas boys were playing outside when one little boy, about 9 years old, hurried into his home and asked his mother, "Mom, how old are you?"

His mom, thought for a moment and replied, "Freddie, there are some things you are not supposed to ask a woman."

"Well, Mom, how much do you weigh?"

"Freddie, that's another of those questions you just don't ask a woman!" she replied as she smiled.

"Mom, I noticed sometimes Daddy sleeps on the couch. Are you two mad at each other?" Freddie particularly wanted an answer to this one.

"Freddie, that is between your daddy and me, now you go outside and play!"

On returning to his friend and telling him what just went on, his friend suggested, "Why don't you go in, look in your Mom's purse and take out her driver's license? All the stuff you wanna know is on her license!"

With that Freddie went in, found his Mom's purse, took out the license, put it back quickly and returned to his friend.

"I did what you told me," stuttered excited little Freddie. "I found out my mom is 33 years old and weighs 124 pounds. I also found out why daddy sometimes sleeps on the couch. Mom made an "F" in sex!"

HE'S SIMPLY NOT AN UP-FRONT KIND OF GUY

Do you remember the nerd from Virginia City, Benny Worthy? When his second year was completed, he decided to stay in Las Vegas a few days and relax by a swimming pool. He got one of those special packages at the Hacienda Hotel/Casino on the strip. These next five days and four nights would serve two purposes. First, he could overcome the stress of taking all those final exams, and two, he could prepare himself for the summer ahead with Barbra Sue. His first couple of days were spent by the pool watching the pretty young girls, admiring their sun tans and their great big smiles. He got no action during that period and was thinking of packing up and heading to VC, when he noticed a sharp looking guy who had a girl on each arm. In fact he was surrounded by girls for most of the time. One day Benny introduced himself to the popular young man.

"I've been watching you and you seem to have a way with women, what is your secret?" asked Benny.

"Here's what I do," replied the young man eager to share his success story. "I take a potato and put it in my swim trunks...that works for me!"

Benny went to the super market closest to the hotel and bought one baking potato, came back to the hotel and placed it in his swim trunks. Two days went by and even though he paraded up and down before some very beautiful young ladies, they did not give him the time of day.

"I did what you told me, I put a potato in my swim trunks and it didn't help me one bit," commented Benny to the young man late one afternoon by the pool.

"Let me give you another tip," smiled the man, "Put the potato in the front!"

W.C. AND HIS RESEARCH

Many years ago, William Claude Dukenfield was visiting Las Vegas enjoying a little rest and relaxation after a busy movie schedule. W.C. Fields, as he was known by his fans worldwide, was walking down Main Street with his bodyguard/bartender strolling dutifully several steps behind him.

Out of nowhere, this great hairy dog comes up to Mr. Fields and takes a leak on his leg. Mr. Fields uttered a string of obscenities that could be heard in Tonopah ending with these instructions: "Driver, go into the nearest emporium and buy me a pound of ground round."

"Mr. Fields, you're not going to feed that animal after he peed on your leg, are you?" quizzed his assistant.

"No, my man, I'm going to find out which end is his mouth and then I'm going to kick him in his ass!"

W.C. GOES FOR IT!

Later that evening, the master comedian crashed a very formal party at the grand opening of the newest casino on the strip, the Riviera Hotel/Casino. This gala affair was attended by stardom and dignitaries from all over the United States. W.C. Fields was there, though without invitation and he was also quite drunk.

He looked across the large ballroom and spied this gorgeous thing in a full length, beautiful green gown. He somehow managed to find his way across the dance floor and asked, "My dear, your pulchritude and charm have transcended the entire length and breadth of this magnificent hall and I have been overcome by your beauty and the beauty of your green gown. May I have this dance?"

"No sir, you may not!" was the curt response.

"May I prevail upon you, my little florabunda, to tell me why you won't do me the honor of this dance?" inquired Mr. Fields.

"For three reasons, sir. Number one is that you are obviously intoxicated. Number two is that this is not a green dress, but a red cassock, and number three is that I am not a woman, I am Joseph O'Mally, Cardinal of Southern California!"

WHERE THERE'S A WILL

Darleen Rose, second shift madam of the 'Silver Spur Ranch' in Lathrop Wells, was a new hire from the Mustang Ranch near Reno. She had lots of experience operating whorehouses in Nevada and always did a good job. The Silver Spur was a series of fenced off double wide trailers housing about twenty "working girls." It did a land office business even though it was some sixty-five long miles north of Las Vegas. There was always a lot of cars parked outside and a lot of traffic inside.

One night a man about 70 years old entered the place and asked for Tamara.

"Sir, Tamara is our most exciting, but also our most expensive girl, are you sure you want her?" asked Darleen.

"Yes, I want Tamara!" repeated the distinguished gentleman.

100

Pretty soon Tamara appeared, had a drink with the gentleman and somewhere in their brief conversation told the man, "Just so you know, I charge $1,000 for each date. Can you handle that?"

The man never blinked and handed the lady ten $100 bills. They went back to her crib and had a reasonably good time.

The next night, Darleen called for Tamara, telling her that the same gentleman who was in the night before was back and was asking for her. The delighted lady happily lead her date back to her room and the two went at it again.

The next night, Tamara was patiently waiting for her senior citizen and gave him a big hug when he came into her small room. They had most excellent close body contact and as he was leaving, she asked, "Are you from around these parts, Daddy?"

"No, Tamara, I'm from Las Vegas," was his reply.

"Is that so. I've got a sister who lives off South Sahara Avenue in Las Vegas," commented Tamara as she zipped up her one piece outfit.

"I know," said the gentleman. "Her name was Janice Allen. I'm her attorney. I'm sorry to tell you Janice died last week, but she instructed me to come up here and personally give you the $3,000 she left you in her will."

A CLOSE RELATIVE

A homeless man was taken by ambulance to Las Vegas Sundown Hospital in Las Vegas with what appeared to be a 'hot' appendix. At the hospital emergency room, the diagnosis was confirmed and the man underwent an emergency appendectomy. When the man comes to in the recovery room a lady asks, "Mr. Douglas, I'm Betty Ridge of the hospital's billing office and I have to ask you some questions. What is the name of your insurance carrier?"

"Lady, I ain't got no insurance!"

"Well, then, can you pay in cash?" asked the lady knowing the answer.

"No, lady, I don't have two coins to rub together!" responded the homeless patient.

"Do you have any close relatives who can help you pay for your care here at the hospital?"

"There's my sister in Reno, but she's a spinster nun," said the man.

Betty Ridge bristled at this and shot back, "Nuns are not spinsters, sir. They're married to God!"

"OK, then," said the man with a smile, "send the bill to my brother-in-law!"

❦

LOCK IT IN!

The growth of Las Vegas over the last twenty years has been phenomenal and, from most indicators will continue to lead the nation for the next decade. Demographers give little hints every so often about this too rapid growth, planning woes, water shortages, traffic snarls, but each time one of those mega-resorts opens its doors you can just figure four employees per room are needed to keep it open.

Is it any wonder that between four and five thousand people are moving into Clark County each month?

This steady influx creates a serious housing problem.

Most try to find apartments, but many buy homes, thus feeding the ever expanding hoard of realtors and their more intelligent cousins...mortgage brokers.

One such mortgage broker, a man about sixty named Charles "Chuck" Collins, had been hacking loans in Las Vegas for about twenty years. He had seen interest rates in the low six's and had seen them...in the early 80's...in the low twenties; the lower rates, not mysteriously, lead to more home purchases and definitely more refinances. The current low interest rate made Chuck about as happy as he ever got.

Chuck was tired and not feeling well. Smoking over two packs of Winstons a day was not helping, nor was his sedentary, but stressful job or his atrocious eating habits. He thought, "If I could only sleep, I'd feel good enough to join a gym and lose forty pounds or so!"

The latter never happened, of course, but the former continued year after year.

One day he was visited in his office by a client...a fiery red-headed Twenty-One dealer named Carmin Stevens who looked ready to kick some major butt.

"Chuck, I told you to lock-in my mortgage interest rate last Tuesday, do you remember that? Here it is Friday and you haven't locked me in yet! I know you haven't because I called and your loan processor said you hadn't gotten to it yet. Look here, you idiot, I know what interest rates have done the last few days and I just know you can't get me that 7.00% rate I wanted on Tuesday. I told you three times to 'Lock in!' What are you going to do about it?"

Nothing Chuck said after that tirade did anything to console this woman. She kept cranking on him, using highly descriptive language and threats. She said she was going to turn him into the Las Vegas Better Business Bureau and to the

Nevada Commerce Department...just for openers!

Somewhere between the curses and the threats, Chuck felt severe chest pain radiating down his left arm. Just before falling out of the leather chair his head hit the corner of the desk; he blacked out momentarily. Curiously, he wondered if he could endure mouth-to-mouth resuscitation from this monstrously ugly woman...not to worry, Chuck!

By the time the paramedics got to the scene little life saving was left to be done. They went through the motions on the way to hospital, but he was thoroughly D.O.A.

Chuck was full of wonderment as he approached the fabled 'Pearly Gates' of Heaven and was greeted by St. Peter.

"Welcome, Charles, I'm Peter, keeper of the gates here at Heaven. Sometimes God Himself greets newcomers, but He is off-campus at an AMA meeting in Chicago. Come, I'll show you around."

The tour took a long, long time and was filled with many wonders. There were whole areas set aside for winged angels praying, others for singing, others for meditating and yet others for playing these golden harps. Chuck was impressed, yet something bothered him.

When the two got back to the check-in area, Chuck asked, "Sir, this is a wonderful place...it's everything I thought it would be, yet I think I'd like to see what the other place...Hell...is like. I'm sure I'll like it better here, but, please won't you let me just take a look?" There was a persuasiveness in his voice, Peter conceded.

At the gates of Hell, Chuck was greeted by a well-dressed man wearing a Georgio Armani suit who looked a little like Al Pacino, but much taller.

"Hello, Chuck! Welcome to Hades. I am the Devil's personal assistant. 'The Man' would have been here

104

personally to show you around, but he's in New York City delivering the key-note address at the annual meeting of the American Bar Association. Follow me and let's take a look around."

After a thorough tour of Hell, Chuck was most impressed. It was nothing like he had pictured. This was one *big party*! There were thousands of beautiful women, a huge 'open' bar, the dancing was sensuous and the casino area stretched for miles and miles...everyone he passed was winning!

"Well, Chuck, what do you think? You've looked at the other place up there, how does it stack up with what you've just seen? asked the number two man.

"Man, I just don't know. It's really great in both places. I'm going to need a day or two to think this over...it's a major decision, you know."

"Yes, it is Chuck. Why don't you take your time. I know you'll make the right choice," smiled the Devil's factotum.

It seemed like an eternity, but after two days and considerable pondering, Chuck had made up his mind. He found himself back at the entrance to Hell talking with the gatekeeper again.

"I've made up my mind, sir. I wish to spend forever right here."

"Splendid! You've made an excellent choice! Let me show you to your quarters," grinned the Turnkey hardly able to contain himself.

Something was wrong! As he walked along he quickly noted the bar was gone, the dancing was gone, the seductive women were no place to be seen. In their places were people screaming while being boiled in oil, others were being beaten with whips and chains, still others were being forced to watch re-runs of 'Gilligan's Island' & 'Vega$.' People were playing bagpipes everywhere!

"Wait just a minute! Two days ago this was a swinging place, everyone was having fun...what's going on here? questioned Chuck.

With a devilish smile, the assistant said, "When you were here two days ago, you should have LOCKED-IN!"

❦

BANDITS IN A GROCERY STORE

The following verse is about a woman from Tennessee who had moved to Las Vegas with her engineer husband, hired to work on the new Bellagio Hotel Casino. She had heard about grocery stores with slot machine areas and wrote the following:

I saw them there, those bandits shine!
And as I shopped, played on my mind.
Had I not wanted to lose dough
Right through that smoky place I'd go.
Want to be here! Assured myself!
Put my groceries on the shelf.
And dropped my quarters one by one
And said out loud, "I'm having fun!"

"Not really fun" offered a man
With dirty quarters in his hand.
Think luck will change? It never does.
It just gets worse! And it's because
These bandits, they are all the same.
They lead you on...they own that game!

So where'd the birthday money go?
The same as all the other dough."

About that time some coins fell fast.
"It's nice, but it can never last.
My hopes get raised with every win!
Luck! At last! Has it changed again?
But no, not mine! Then come the tears
For Bandit's theft through all the years.
Many nice things could have been done
With all that money never won!"

I'd put about four dollars in
And scored only one little win.
Scooped them all up, the few coins left.
Allow no more on-going theft!
'Good-Luck' to the man sitting there
Smoking, lost in a vacant stare.
He's getting very far behind.
Bandit slots...they will steal your mind!

Argeepee

ON AND OFF CAMPUS

It happens every home game of the Running Rebels, the mighty UNLV football team. Revelers, mostly students, former students and people who actually need an excuse to get drunk, gather in the parking lot of the stadium. Police are thankful it only happens five or six times each year. There are motor homes, trucks, station wagons and vans loaded with beer, food, beer, barbecues and beer—tail gaters! Sometimes revelers just go ahead and skip the ball game.

At this particular game between the Rebels and the Rams of the University of California-Silicon Valley, Jack, a sophomore (or less) majoring in beer and amateur gynecology, was sitting with three buddies drinking beer around a card table telling jokes and sharing highly confidential information about their last dates.

The quartet took turns going to the porta-potties set up for all these beer processors. Jack noticed that each time he used the facility, on returning, his beer was all gone. Of course, no one owned up to drinking his brew, so Jack would just pop another one. After a couple of hours of this, Jack's cooler of Brewsky's was nearly empty. Before panic set in, Jack printed a note on a piece of paper he would put over his beverage next time he had to go, which could be any time now.

On returning and feeling confident his beer would be as he left it, Jack could see at a distance his cup was still there and his note was still there. He sat down grinning, and, as he began to slip the note in his pocket for future use, he noticed there was other writing on it. Near the place where Jack had printed in bold letters...'I spit in this beer!' were smaller letters, "So did I!"

❦

CAN'T WE ALL JUST GET ALONG?

Another variation on the above story takes place on an airplane headed to Reno from Las Vegas. Three UNLV students are going to Reno for a Friday night basketball game between the Wolfpack and the Running Rebels. Two of the students are UNLV football players and big ones at that. Each goes about 275 pounds and neither fits comfortable in the small seats of the Southwest plane.

The two football players were friends, but had not met the small student who was sitting between them. After introductions they settled back for the one hour flight. The smallish guy in the middle commented it would be good to get home again for a long weekend. The fireworks started!

They began to berate the little guy, exhibiting a surprisingly high degree of animus against him. They let it be known that he was not welcome in Las Vegas and he should be going to school in Reno where he belonged.

When the cabin attendant came along, the two ball players ordered orange juice while the Renoite ordered a cup of coffee. The big dudes finished their juice about the same time and began anew their attacks on the poor guy in the middle. Some pretty awful things were said to and about the young man culminating in their ordering him to get up and get them some more OJ. It took him about five minutes. He came back and gave them their juice, which they drank down in two gulps. He heard the two boys snickering as he noticed they had spit in his coffee. The attendant came by, he got a fresh cup which lasted until they got to the Reno-Tahoe International Airport. As they were walking toward the main gate, he commented.

"Guys, this rivalry between UNR and UNLV has got to stop! As far as I am concerned, it has gone too far as it is. It's actually ridiculous! Do you know what I mean? First it's football. Then it's basketball. Then it's academics. Then it's 'You spit in my coffee.' And then it's 'I pee in your orange juice!'"

❦

A FAMILY TREE WITH NO BRANCHES!

Arnold was very interested in learning about his family tree. He ordered and read about a half dozen books on heraldry, heritage and family histories. He was at the point of having a multi-colored coat of arms drawn up by the professionals down on the Maryland Parkway in Las Vegas.

At the shop, he visited briefly with a very polite woman who chatted about his surname and showed him some examples of what could be his family crest. She collected as much information as he could give and he departed.

When he returned in six weeks, she showed him a beautiful crest with dancing dolphins, rearing lions and some wheat sheaths; red, gold, and silver were his colors. He asked, "What is this inscription at the bottom...looks like Latin?"

"Yes, sir, it is Latin. 'Envidet Menor Est' is your family's motto. It means, 'He who envies is a lesser man!'"

Arnold was very pleased. He paid the lady and went to the closest framing shop and had a very expensive frame made for his prized coat of arms, took it home and hung it over his fireplace. Gosh, was he proud of it!

Over the next several days he began to think about the family motto and decided to convert the Latin to English. However, he asked himself, was it politically correct to say "He who envies is a lesser man?" No, it was not.

Arnold began what turned out to be an exercise in stupid! He became obsessed with developing alternatives that would be 'with it!' Right for the times, more P.C., the following were revised 'mottoes' he reviewed.

"Lesser is he who envies" while one 'gender indicator' is eliminated there is still one left that annoyed him.

"Lesser is he or she who envies." Too pedantic!

"Lesser is the person who envies." Too bland!

"Diminished is that individual who envies the accomplishments, wealth, good looks, intelligence, life-position, or whatever of another individual." Arnold was an attorney, but no, not this one either.

"An envier is lessened." Not bad!

"An envier is diminished." Even better!

"Enviers are minimized." Nope!

Arnold even threw in an 'Ebonics' thought prevalent in the Oakland, CA. school district at that time.

"Dissed bees de dude who want de shit of some other home boy!"

After this exercise, Arnold changed his newly acquired family motto to:

"An envier is diminished."

111

BE CAREFUL WHAT YOU ASK

The Las Vegas Metropolitan Police are a distinguished group. They made the TV show 'Vega$' a hit for several years and they are at work today. Just the other night, Officer Stanley was patrolling an area south of town where complaints were coming in about people parking, drinking beer and trashing the place. There was even some talk about sexual activity taking place. This was reported to the police by an old lady with a pair of binoculars.

Sgt. Stanley came upon a car with no visible occupants. This could mean two things, there was no one in the car, or it could mean that some of that alleged sexual activity was taking place. He approached the vehicle with his right hand on his holster and his left hand grasping that fifteen inch flashlight. He shined it in the car and, predictably, two heads popped up from the back seat. The policeman asked as he flashed his badge;

"Just what do you think you're doing back there?"

"Officer," said the young man, "I'm boffing my girlfriend back here!"

Appreciating the boy's honesty and wanting to depart a little humor before he sent them on, he asked, "That's great, mind if I take a turn?"

"That would be great, officer, but I never boffed a policeman before!"

❦

CHURCH MUSIC

With over a million people living in Clark County there has to be a story or two about children. This one is about two little boys who lived in the shadows of the big casinos just off the strip. One of the boys about six years old was so proud of his canary he took him to school, to the play ground and to his friend's home.

One day the canary died and the two boys, after a few tears, decided to give the little bird a proper funeral. They went in the back yard, dug a small hole, wrapped the bird in a napkin, covered him and made a little cross out of popsickle sticks. One of the boys said.

"I've seen people on TV say prayers when someone is buried, do you know any prayers?"

"I think so, I used to live near a Catholic Church," said the little boy. They knelt, folded their hands and the little guy said "Under the 'B'...fifteen, under the 'N'...forty five..."

❧

NO BULL!

There was this guy who lived in a very nice section of town called Vegas Valley and he used to walk his pit bull terrier each evening about dusk.

On more than one occasion he would sic his dog on other unsuspecting canines and totally demolish them. The Humane Society had been notified and he had been warned to cease and desist this inhumane activity but he ignored them.

One of the animal control people, a guy named Bert Drover, became aware of this man's deeds and decided to do something about it. He watched the pit bull owner for several days and learned his dog-walking routine.

One evening, the man was walking his aggressive pet when he spied our man Bert across the street with a small yellow animal on a leash. He leaned over, unhitched his dog and said "Sic, 'em!"

The pit bull ran across the street, attacked the smaller animal and in an instant the fight was over. There was no more pit bull...vanished...chomp!

The distraught pit bull owner hurried across the street in disbelief, swearing at the owner of the other dog as he went.

"What in hell have you done with my dog? What kind of animal is that to eat my dog that quick?"

Bert Drover grinned a little and said, "Before I cut his tail off and painted him yellow, he was an alligator!"

FISH PUN

The new Mirage Hotel Casino hired Ron Brown to be the keeper of the Dolphins...a valued attraction at the Mega-Bucks Las Vegas strip property.

Ron was proud of his Dolphins, teaching them complicated tricks and gestures like counting to five with air blast out of their blow holes. They were almost as smart, thought Ron, as his adult children.

As he experimented with diets, training, personal attention, care and handling, Ron learned his Dolphins had a keen interest in eating sea gulls. After extensive physical examination, Ron learned that by eating sea gulls, his pets could actually extend their lives. They could extend their lives, he was sure, indefinitely. This prospect excited him no end, and he spent his afternoons going to Lake Mead and capturing sea gulls for his experiments.

One day after being at the lake all day collecting sea gulls, he returned to the Mirage with several birds tucked under his arms. In the middle of the path leading back to the arena where the Dolphins were anxiously waiting for him, was a sleeping lion. Being very careful not to awaken the lion, Ron stepped over him and went on down the path. With that, four representatives of the Metropolitan Police force arrested him, read him his rights and took him to jail.

At the arraignment, Ron asked why he was arrested and why he was being detained.

"Sir, the charges against you," curtly replied the Assistant District Attorney, "are 'Transporting Gulls Across A Staid Lion For Immortal Porpoises!'"

CAT SHOES

The Siegfried and Roy act on the Las Vegas strip has been described as a wonder of this world. They make the strip come alive with their feats of Legerdemain...to those of you in Lida Junction, that's magic, slight of hand, illusion. They can make anything disappear...pretty girls go "poof"...cars vanish, large cats go away. That's their specialty...large cats and they have a collection of exotic felines that would make any zoo in the world envious.

Their home, make that walled castle-fortress, it is rumored, has been designed to allow these huge cats to roam freely...no restrictions. This has caused problems on several occasions.

For example, Roy had recently bought an expensive pair of shoes to be used in the act, and, without thinking, had left them on the patio one night. The next morning he went to look for them and yes, they were gone. He informed his staff and the search began.

Roy located his shoes in the grasp of his largest, very possessive white tiger. He knew the only way he could retrieve them was by calling his vet and having the big cat tranquilized. The vet came, darted the beast and loaded him onto a wheelbarrow.

As the vet wheeled the tiger back to the house with Roy walking beside him, Siegfried quizzed him from the balcony.

"Pardon Me, Roy, Is That The Cat That Chewed Your New Shoes?"

❦

SIGNING

Anthony James was one of the best and most honest managers in the counting room of the huge Las Vegas Grand Temple Casino. He had been there several years and he could look forward to many more years with the firm. So, why did he draw that automatic and clean out the place one evening? He quietly walked out the employees entrance, got into his car and drove away.

Guido Armano, a trustworthy soldier was directed to find Mr. James and was given his whereabouts...a trailer park in Laughlin, Nevada. He was told to get the money and do anything to effect that end. He took along with him a soldier named Salvador Delgedice who had some skill in American Sign Language. Our thief, Mr. James was a deaf mute.

116

It was over 110 degrees in the shade when they reached the overcrowded trailer park in Laughlin...and there was no shade. They located the thief and Guido told Salvador to tell the man the following:

"Tell him that I know he stole the money and that I have come for it. Tell him not to give me any sob story. All I want is the money and I'll go away."

Delgedice passed this information to James who looked stunned. He signed back to Sal and then Sal told Guido, "He says he don't know what you are talking about, he don't have no money."

"Listen, Sal, tell him I mean him no harm...all I want is the $50,000 he stole and we will be square."

Again, Salvador relayed Guido's thoughts and received a great deal of signing back.

"Boss, this guy says he ain't got a clue what you are talking about. Their ain't no money as far as he is concerned."

This time Guido took out a big black forty-five revolver, cocked it and aimed it right between the eyes of Mr. James saying, "Sally, tell Mr. James here that if I don't get the money immediately, I will blow his head completely off his stupid body!"

Sally relayed this mandate and Mr. James, after having the situation 'splained' to him, relented. He signed to Sal, "Hey, give me a break, guys. I been working for the casino a long time, never took a dime. I figure the club owed me the money. The money is buried in a coffee can in the side yard over by the rose bed."

Salvador, grasping the situation quickly told Guido. "This guy must be nuts. You wanna know what he told me? He said you looked like a dumb WOP bastard and sure, he got the dough, but he ain't giving it up to no Dago lookin' son of a bitch like you. What's more he said you ain't got the balls to shoot him either!"

🦂

NEAR THE END

It was a slow night in the precinct covering north Las Vegas when this very intoxicated man stumbles in, catches himself, and approaches the desk sergeant.

"Ossifer, I want to report that my car has been stolen!" It took some time for the man to get all those words out in that order.

"Sir, what makes you think your car has been stolen?" asked the sergeant.

With that the drunk produced a set of keys, pointed a key at the officer and said, "I know it's been stolen 'cause the last time I looked, my car was right on the end of this key!"

The sergeant smiled a little thinking that this could happen. Then he noticed the man was dressed haphazardly with his fly open and his private parts were hanging out. He directed the man to fix himself up, make himself presentable.

The man putting his shirt back into his pants, cinching up his belt and looking down at his privates all hanging out, shouted, "Oh, No! They stole my girlfriend, too!"

RENO...IT COULD HAVE BEEN SPELLED "RENAULT"

RENO...IT COULD HAVE BEEN SPELLED "RENAULT"

Reno is situated at the foot of the Sierra Nevada mountains in the northwestern portion of the Sagebrush State, also called the Silver State. It embodies about as much history as there is Nevada and that is not much.

Reno was named for Attorney General Janet Reno who was an appointee of President Bill Clinton. NO! Actually, it was named for a Yankee General Jesse L. Reno who came west to civilize the territory and other worthwhile reasons. He stayed here long enough to cause this dusty little river town to be named after him. He then went back east and got himself killed in an obscure Civil War skirmish. Those who know say the general's parents spelled their name 'Renault,' but changed it to Reno to keep people from thinking their family was connected with the family that would eventually build that horrible little car. People in Hawthorn, Nevada to this day still pronounce the name of the car 'Ree-nalt!'

The city of Sparks was named after a former governor who was batting around northern Nevada around the turn of the century. There was no Las Vegas to speak of at that time. There used to be an expression...still is, I guess, "Reno is so close to Hell you can see sparks." Some would wonder if the phrase referred to the late governor.

Reno is only about an inch away from Lake Bigler on most

121

maps. Lake Bigler, or, as some people prefer to call it, 'Lake Tahoe,' is about a third in Nevada and the rest in California. California government never misses an opportunity to remind us of this fact. Except for Lake Titicaca somewhere in Peru, Lake Tahoe is the largest and deepest lake at 6,200 feet on the planet. (Now, what do you think of that?) It's so clear you can read the government warning on a beer can, 45 feet below the surface.

President Clinton and his band of merry people visited Tahoe recently and made a lot of noise about preserving the lake 'for future generations' and that is a good idea!

The spillway for Tahoe is the mighty Truckee River. Reno and Sparks and a lot of communities in northern Nevada receive benefits from the water that comes out. Californians do not like it one bit that two thirds of the lake belongs to them but all the water that flows out of it flows into Nevada and eventually evaporates in Pyramid Lake. That water could be used by Los Angelans to flush toilets.

In past years, the Paiute Indian Nation, located in northern Nevada has done everything it legally can think of to prevent Reno and Sparks from using any of the Truckee River water that passes through it. They say the huge Pyramid Lake, which is fed entirely by that river, is drying up due to all that drinking and flushing going on up stream. Periodically, one of a host of courts involved in this dispute makes a ruling and one side or the other gets pissed.

If one of these courts was to rule that these populated areas could use all the water they wanted, then Pyramid Lake would surely turn into a pea-soup brine and die. Conversely, if a court rules all the water must run into the lake and disappear like it has been doing for millions of years, then there would be no Reno and no Sparks.

Were one to attempt a comparison between Reno/Sparks and Las Vegas, that would be a feckless task. For good or ill, the two areas don't yield to comparison.

Reno and Sparks people are convinced they're just plain better than Las Vegans. They have more history, more culture, are better educated and have better attitudes about nearly everything. They can't explain away the world class basketball teams occasionally produced by UNLV.

Las Vegans, on the other hand, feel they are the real Nevadans. They proclaim there are no pretenses about why they are screwing around in the desert. They escaped from someplace else, to move to this flat, alkaline, brutally hot, fast paced, entertainment intense metropolis: *To make as much money as fast as possible and quickly return to wherever they came from.* Sure, there's a university (and a good one, too!), other centers of learning, an opera, an orchestra, maybe even a ballet? But the real reason for being there has just been stated. No pretenses!

Having said that then, what are the dreams of northern Nevadans? Who knows! People I talk with seem always to be in anticipation that something good is going to happen; waiting on something. Waiting on the ski season to open, or the city or county to fix the pot holes, waiting on a decision to tear down or renovate the old Mapes Hotel, waiting for the governor and the attorney general to do something about the unconscionably high cost of gasoline, waiting on the legislature to begin, or better, waiting on it to finally end, waiting on the regional planning agency to approve another outrageous housing or gaming project...waiting!!

North and Cow County legislators are waiting, too. They are waiting for the sleeping lion in the south to begin to roar. They are waiting for Clark County...Las Vegas...to finally get its political act together and virtually take over the entire operations of the state. There was talk once of moving the capitol (Carson City) to Las Vegas. That may not be such a bad idea if you think it through.

Reno and the other fifteen counties firmly held the power in this state for over 100 years. Most think northerners did a pretty good job with the power. Others think northerners screwed the state for all time and suggest "Let the torch be passed to a new generation!" OK by me so long as all the new generations will not be Californians! Northerners strongly suspect, however, that most of that new generation will be Californians!

IT'S MINE...IT'S RENO

Glowing, little town on the river.
It's Reno here where gaming is king.
My home, my high desert oasis,
It's mine, I helped make it...it's Reno!

Nevada! Discover Nevada!
The Silver State right now in it's prime.
"Biggest Little City" North...Shining!
It's mine, I helped make it...it's Reno!

Reno, wedded to the Sierra.
Quite secure in it's place in the state.
My home, my jewel in the desert,
It's mine, I helped make it...it's Reno!

Argeepee

❦

LIBRARY SCIENCE

It wasn't every day that Charles Mandlee, Assistant Administrator for Washoe County Library System saw a chicken come through the doors of the main branch. And it wasn't everyday a chicken came up to his desk, jumped up on the desk and said,

"Blook?"

Now, Chuck was nobody's fool. He could tell instantly this was a highly intelligent chicken, but just to make sure he'd heard correctly he asked,

"What was that?"

"Blook!" the chicken responded somewhat emphatically.

"I see," said Chuck, "You want a book!" With that he slipped a book under the chicken's wing.

The white bird hopped down from the desk and walked calmly through the theft detectors and out the door.

Mr. Mandlee became awfully busy and this little episode, while not forgotten, was put on the back burner for half an hour. As he looked up from his papers, here comes the white fowl again. Was he returning the book so soon, thought Chuck?

The chicken stood there in front of the Assistant Librarian for a long while then jumped on his desk and dropped the book. The bird then clucked.

"Blook! Blook!"

Chuck knew exactly what to do and slipped a book under each wing. As the bird left the building, Chuck knew he had to follow. The bird went north on Center Street moving at a leisurely pace and walked down to the Truckee River. Chuck followed at a safe distance.

There sitting on a rock was a large bullfrog basking in the sun. The chicken hopped on the rock and dropped the books. Chuck watched in amazement as the frog looked at one book, then the other and said, "Read it! Read it!"

BLACK IS BEAUTIFUL

They were Rabbis at last. The schooling was as interminable as it was rewarding and fulfilling, but they were Rabbis now!

Josh and David now had to buy proper attire. At the synagogue on Lakeside Drive in Reno, they were told to go to Pincus The Tailor over on South Virginia Street.

At the shop, Mr. Pincus was pleased to see Josh and Dave and took them back to the fitting room for measurements, one of the overhead bulbs in the already dimly lit room was out which made Pincus's deception all the better. He did not have black suits in stock.

He brought out two dark blue serge suits and fitted them to the two men. Josh questioned whether or not these suits were black. But was assured by Pincus they were. The jackets fit perfectly...40 regular...and 38 short...and the pants only need inseam stitching. Within thirty-five minutes, the two were out the door.

Josh was still uncertain about the color of his new suit and he caused David to become equally concerned. It was a cloudy day, the sun wasn't helping much.

There was an Episcopal Diocesan convention being held in Reno at that time, and two Anglican nuns were doing a

126

little sight seeing.

The Rabbis took note of this and David suggested,

"Josh, we know nuns wear black, don't we? Why don't you strike up a conversation with the sisters and I'll move close enough to make a good comparison of their black habits and whatever it is we are wearing."

Josh greeted the ladies and chatted them up for a few minutes about their having recently become Rabbis and being new to Reno. David was not too obvious about his color comparison activity. The foursome departed with kind words.

As the nuns walked away, one of the sisters commented.

"Isn't it wonderful sister Marguerite, the way our Jewish brothers are embracing the ecumenical spirit in their teaching institutions?"

"Sister Mary, whatever do you mean?"

Sister Mary replied, "I mean the way they are teaching Latin in their schools!"

"I still don't understand," said Sister Marguerite.

"Why, Sister, I distinctly heard one of the Rabbis, the short one, speak Latin when they walked away. He said, 'Pincus screwdus, Pincus screwdus.'"

MEDIUM WELL-DONE ROAST

"Ladies and Gentlemen, friends of Mayor Timothy Clary, thank you for coming tonight to help us send the Mayor out of office and out of this state. I am Rick Allen, your master of ceremonies for the night. As you know, the Mayor did not offer for re-election to office back in November and since that time he has accepted a lucrative job elsewhere. This looks

127

like a real win/win doesn't it? We get rid this bum and he gets honest work!

"Tonight we have a treat for you. Four former friends of the mayor are going to skewer him, cook him over a hot fire and serve him up to you. We only hope the mayor doesn't get mad and leave sooner than he had planned, we already paid for his dinner! Here goes.

"Our first roaster is Barry Ryland. He comes to us by way of the Nevada State Pen maximum security...where he has been serving an indeterminate sentence for being criminally inept and terminally ordinary. Put your hands together for Barry Ryland!

"OK, Rick, you said you would go easy on me...I now intend to send the press and your wife those picture of you in the middle of that three way with those sheep! See me after the program and I'll still give you a good price on the negatives.

"But enough about Tom and those two gorgeous ewes. We're here to have some fun at Mayor Tim's expense.

"Tim, we're going to miss you...will miss your pointless speeches, silly proclamations, your endless diatribes at council meetings and your tiresome dissertations on what to do with all those pot holes!

"We will miss your simple smile! We know it kept you out of numerous fist fights on City Council. Other council members knew it was bad karma to hit mentally retarded people.

"I've done my homework on this one. Few people know that Tim is a native Nevadan raised in Hawthorn, Nevada. He told me recently that the hardest three years in his life were spent in the third grade. But he has been a supporter of education: he's always been very bright...for example:

"When asked if two plus three *is* or *are* six, he proudly states that two plus three definitely *is* six!

"When he was asked, "Who shot Jack Kennedy?" he said there was a witness that would swear he was at the Mustang Ranch that day!

"Who had a very nice job before he became mayor...had over 1,000 people under him? He cut grass at the cemetery over on Stoker Avenue.

"Who thinks the town of Lovelock was named after a sexual position?

"Who ran a red light over at Plumb and South Virginia, but made up for it by sitting through two green lights on Kietzke Lane later that same day?

"Who was graduated from the University of Nevada, Reno, with a degree in mathematics? Said he was proud of cramming two years of study into eight years of college.

"Whose motto is 'never tell a lie unless it is absolutely convenient'?

"Who never was bothered by adversity...other people's adversity, that is?

"Who has all the confidence of a Christian with four aces?

"Who never did anything wrong while other people were watching?

"I could go on for several more minutes on the attributes of his honor the Mayor, but I think I will leave the rest of my time to the bard, the wordsman from Stratford on Avon (No! Tim, that's not a town near Austin, Nevada!) That great sculptor of prose...Shakespeare. Listen for the message. I'm certain you will know he was talking about our own Tim Clary:

'Ever has the quintessence of spirituality bestowed upon such a brow as this...nay, nay thou dastardly villain which hideth in the shadow of outrageous misadventure upon, above, below that great tribute which passeth this hour. When we shall partake of this truth...great arbitrator of justice? Speak, speak, lest thou miss the moment and forever be separated from that jubilation...alas, alas, and harken...the time has come to know and in knowing consult the fullness. Be not deterred by marking time and treading not upon that dark frontier lest thou goest unreproached!!!'

"What else can be said! How about a hand for the bard! Thank you folks!"

"Hey, how about the Bard and how about Barry? Your comments and especially the words of Shakespeare were truly meaningless," offered the M.C.

"On the agenda now is some chicken soup...no, I mean the next speaker is Betty Stronach Marcy. Betty has been a fixture at events such as this for years and we are all eagerly awaiting her thoughts on the passing of Mayor Tim...Betty..."

"Rick, you always do such a truly marginal job as Master of Ceremonies; I am honored to be here...however. I could have been home sorting my socks, but, no...here I am. By the way, Tom, why didn't you read the introduction I wrote for you? That's right, I forgot...you were socially promoted at Reno High and never learned to read the big words.

"Let's talk about Tim...our beloved Mayor.

"I was wondering, Mr. Mayor who your role models were when you were growing up? Were they really the Three Stooges and Zippo Marx? That's right you threw in Sen. Strom Thurmond too, didn't you?"

"Few people knew that Tim was in that courageous group of men who raised the flag on Iwo Jima. Unfortunately, this happened during the Viet Nam conflict.

"What can be said about Tim, that hasn't already been said

about Bill Clinton who redefined sexual intercourse, about Jimmy Carter, who showed us verbal restraint after hitting his thumb with a hammer, about Ronald McDonald who demonstrated for 30 years, that you *can* make a hamburger without meat? What can be said about Tim that he hasn't already said about himself?

"But really folks, a lot of people who do interesting things never get roasted.

"Chick Hecht, our former U.S. Senator who called the Yucca Mountain site a 'nuclear suppository,' never got a roast like this.

"Priscilla Ford, the lady who ran down all those people on South Virginia Street sent a card to Tim saying 'Sorry I missed you on Thanksgiving,' she never got a roast!

"Charlie Mapes, who left us with an old dilapidated building we can't sell, renovate or tear down...never got a roast!

"Janet Dalsky, former city council woman who said... 'Show me the money,' then spent it, and split Reno...never got a roast!

"Tad Dunbar, Channel 8 News anchor, who, if he gains one more pound can hire out as the Goodyear blimp...he never got a roast!

"But Tim gets a roast, and I'm happy to be one of the chefs! Thanks!"

"My goodness, Betty! You're doing so much better!! Your psychiatrist tells me you're allowed visitors at Lake's Crossing now. They're waiting outside to take you back after the program.

"Next on the grill is retired restaurant owner Eugene Klaus who will continue cooking our guest."

"Thanks you, M.C. Rick, I am truly uninspired by the

speakers who have gone before me and I wanna know before I go any further, when do I get my money? This thing could bomb out any minute now. While I'm up here let me tell you what Mark Twain would have said about Tim if he were here.

"The Creator made idiots, morons, and imbeciles...that was for practice...then He made this retiring mayor!

"If Tim's ignorance, stubbornness, and poor judgement were spun into a fine thread, it would circle the globe 16 times and tie!

"If you take a poor dog and make him prosperous he will not bite you. That is the principle difference between a dog and Tim Clary!

"Enough about Mr. Twain; there is so much more I want to say about this forgettable person, Tim Clary...but I forgot it all...

"What I really want to say is that I have been influenced greatly by Tim. I have seen what a life of lying, cheating, thieving and debauchery have done to him and I have quit most of those things. My life is truly boring and I hate him for changing my life!

"What can you say about Tim that hasn't already been said about hemorrhoids, root canals and vasectomies?

"I can't go on anymore! My mom always told me, when you can't think of nice things to say about someone, it's time to shut the hell up! Thanks, Mom!"

"Thanks, Gene...you were almost adequate that time...keep trying, huh? How did he get on the program anyway? I heard funnier lines at Mother Theresa's funeral!

"Our last roaster is none other than Phil Phillips. As none of you know, Phil owns and makes a huge profit on some of the sleaziest fast food and fuel stores in northern Nevada. His motto is "Eat at Phil's and get free gas!" Ladies and gentlemen, let's hear it for our last roaster, Phil Phillips."

"Thanks, Rick, I forgive you for that contemptible introduction, but thanks for the plug for my stores. My wife thought up a raffle idea! We have a special on Fridays, with a tank of gas everyone has a chance to win free sex. Owners and employees can win, too! I haven't won yet, but my wife has already won four times! Gees! Some people have all the luck...but enough about luck...we're here to give Tim a warm send off. Are the guys with the blow torches ready to come on? Just kidding, Tim!

"Rick, do you remember the last time you were asked to introduce someone? I have waited until now to say you did a pretty good job, but you made some minor mistakes. It wasn't the speaker, it was his brother. It wasn't gold, it was silver, and he didn't make five million. He lost five million. Other than that, you nailed that introduction! I just thought you ought to know...

"What gives with Mayor Tim, anyway? He gives all this up so he can get a job paying more than minimum wage. Who did that wonderful facial surgery on you over the last four years? It hid your wrinkles, took care of that double chin you were developing and it allows you to speak out of both sides of your mouth at the same time like good politicians should be able to do.

"I heard they're putting two new faces on Mt. Rushmore this year...both of them yours!

"Your critiques say you ought to buy the Mustang Ranch Brothel...it's up for sale again, you know...you've been doing that sort of things to your constituents for almost four years now anyway!

"You've heard that song Cher sings, *Gypsies, Tramps, and Thieves?* Cher wrote it after observing the city council for half an hour.

"It was nice of you to buy your wife a new bathing suit for her birthday, Tim. After all, the last one you bought her does have a hole in the knee!"

"When you heard your wife wanted a watch for Christmas, you let her.

"Yes, Tim, we heard your wife bought you a toupee because she heard you were getting balled at the office!

"Your wife told me you bought one of those cheap hair pieces out of a magazine. She didn't know what kind of hair it was, but every time you pass a fire hydrant, one of the sideburns lifts up!

"Tim, it was a happy time for us when you were elected to office four years ago. Everyone here tonight voted for you, we know that, but the Registrar of Voters—we get a new one after each election—said you were really popular! People have come back from the dead to vote for you!

"Just remember, if you see a yellow Rider truck outside your house or office that smells sorta funny...clear out the house...and don't call any of us to help you!

"Good luck, Mr. Mayor...thank you, Mr. MC!"

"No, thank you, Phil, for what might be the best of a sorry bunch of roasters. Honestly, when you pay $22.00 for these performances you expect to get your money's worth.

"He has sat there, smiling occasionally, wincing a couple of times...now it's his turn. Let's hear it for the roastee, the honorable Tim Clary!"

"I will be brief, ladies and gentlemen. There were times

tonight I wanted to cry...throw up first...then cry. I never knew so many people cared so little for me. How about the nerve of those people anyway...I never liked any of them either!

"That first roaster, Barry, I think I represented him when I was with the public defender's office. He was arrested for flashing at Meadowood mall. Barry was released to his family who tried to get him into therapy. There was agreement at first, but later Barry decided to stick it out another six months!

"Barry tried poetry after doing a year in county jail. I attended a reading of his works and distinctly remember the following idiotic rendering.

'Last night I held a beautiful hand.
I could hear the angels sing.
I was the happiest in all the land.
Four aces and a king!'

"What do you think...sucks, doesn't it?

"Then there was Betty! I hope they don't let that girl out again for a long time! She had a scam a while back where she convinced people to invest in a business to raise rats to feed to cats, which would be skinned for their fur. After skinning by welfare moms on a federal grant, the cats would be fed to the rats thus completing the no-overhead cycle. Only problem was she couldn't find a market for the fur. She did sell a few rat pelts to Phil Phillips for a new toupee, however!

"Gene Klaus, you never give up, do you? Is there nothing you won't do for a free meal and a seat at the head table? Talk about a grifter!! Gene was arrested by the bunko squad last week when he tried to scam Chief Kirkfield who was working under cover.

"Pst, do you want to buy the bones of the Elephant Man?" he said. To which the chief astutely replied,

"Hey, those bones are already in a museum in London!"

"Yeh, but these are the Elephant Man's bones when he was a child!"

"Actually, Gene got a very good price for them: The Chief was happy, too!

"What about that Phil Phillips! He had the nerve to reuse the same material I used on him at his roast five years ago. Phil, don't you have any shame? I guess not, Phil considers himself an idea man. During the second world war, Phil said he had a way to stop the German subs from sinking all those ships. Just boil the water and when the subs came to the top, sink them! Someone asked him how he thought the ocean could be boiled: he replied,

"I have the idea. You work out the details!"

"I want to get my hands on the people who brought all these people together for a left-handed tribute to me on my leaving office, and to top it all off, they put that idiot Rick...what's his name?...in charge of it all!

Just remember, what goes around, comes around! I may be back someday and when and if I do, I'm going to stalk each and every one of you who had anything to do with this charade!

"For some obscure reason, I want to thank all of you for the effort put into this event. Nothing happens by itself and I am pleased with all the negative attention. In closing, I want to quote that same Mark Twain when he interviewed a man who had just been tarred and feathered and run out of Virginia City on a greased rail. Twain, a reporter at the time, asked the man what he thought of it.

"Except for the honor in it," replied the man, "I would just as soon forgo it!"

"Thank you, although I will try to forget it, I will always remember this night and you, my friends!"

❦

AN EXPENSIVE QUESTION

For many years the legendary Bill Harrah, gaming pioneer, auto collector and major employer in the Reno area operated a 'Rolls Royce' dealership on Fourth Street. This was a strange sight. A town of 40,000 people with a 'Rolls' dealership.

Folks would come to town, visit the clubs, catch the shows, eat the inexpensive food, get married or divorced or whatever, then walk over to see the latest Rolls on Harrah's showroom floor. It was quite a draw to the city. Only a handful of people around today can tell if he actually sold any of those expensive cars, but it was an inspiration to the gamblers to think someone might actually win enough money to buy one. Picture this, a visitor from, say, Lovelock, Nevada is in town for the weekend and, to kill a little time, walks over to look at a car he can only dream of owning. Sometimes during his observation he must ask the salesman, "How much gas mileage does this car get?"

The salesman, having heard this many, many times over the years must respond by saying, "Sir, if you have to ask that dumb ass question, you can't afford this car!"

❦

137

SMART ANSWERING

Jerry Stovall was a very good airplane mechanic, but he never could keep a job. It seems he was always too flip with the customers and they would complain to the boss and next thing you know, Jerry was sacked.

Jerry had been at Reno Flight Services for two months, which was about as long as he stayed anyplace when the boss said he wanted to see him in his office. Jerry knew what was coming.

"Jerry, you're a very good mechanic, but you are running off all my good customers with your sarcastic comments. I'm going to have to let you go, you'll be paid through the end of the month. Good luck!"

To that, Jerry asked "What's going on? I just started work here last month! What's the beef?"

The bossman opened Jerry's file and began to read Jerry's comments on a collection of work orders.

Problem: Airplane radio has an unbelievably loud hum.
Your comments: Radio hum reset to a more believable level!

Problem: Friction locks cause throttle levers to stick.
Your comments: That's what the hell they are there for!

Problem: Something loose in cockpit.
Your comments: Something tightened in cockpit!

Problem: The autopilot doesn't.
Your comments: Now it does!

Problem: Left tire almost needs replacement.
Your comments: Left tire almost replaced!

Problem: Evidence of hydraulic leak on right landing gear.
Your comments: Evidence removed!

Problem: Number two engine missing.
Your comments: Number two engine located on wing after brief search!

Problem: Computerized autoland program caused very rough landing.
Your comments: Autoland computer program not installed on this aircraft.

The boss closed the file and said, "Come back to see me when you have adjusted your attitude."

THE MISSING TEN SPOT

The Silver Leprosy Hotel Casino in the heart of Reno had just opened when three men from San Francisco came in wanting a room. The desk clerk was eager to sell the last room, a suite, and, talking to the men and to the bellhop at the same time said, "Let's see...three gentlemen have just taken the last room in the house, a beautiful suite, for one night...at three hundred dollars." Without objection each man threw in a crisp hundred dollar bill. They were taken to their room.

The desk clerk realized about twenty minutes later he had made a serious mistake that would go on his record if not corrected. He had charged $300 for a suite that goes for $250. He called the bellman over and gave him five ten dollar bills to return to the guests.

On the way up to the room, the bellman did a little figuring. It would cause trouble if he gave three men five ten dollar bills to divvy up. He put two tens in his pocket and give each man a ten dollar bill. They were happy. Having done this he went back to the bell stand and did some more math. "Let's see," he said, "the room was $300 and each man paid $100. Each got back $10. That means each paid $90. Right? So, if three men paid $90 each...that's $270...and I kept $20, that's $290. Where did the other $10 go?"

The bellhop, in later years ran for state treasurer of Nevada and won!

❦

COMPARISON

A man came home with a black eye after doing some shopping at one of Reno's several very good bookstores. He had been listening to Howard Stern...the outrageous Mr. Stern...on the radio and decided to buy Howard's book *Private Parts*.

His wife asked, "What in the world happened to you? How did you get that shiner?"

"I was over at Barony's Books, did a little browsing, picked up Howard's book and got in line to pay for it...I noticed that this little guy in front of me was also buying the same book, and I don't know if it was the light or the way he was holding it, but his book appeared smaller than mine. I asked, "Pardon me, sir, let's compare our *Private Parts*. I

think my *Private Parts* is bigger and thicker than yours. Tell
you what, let's put our *Private Parts* on the counter, get a
ruler and measure them."
   "With that, the little guy grabbed his "Private Parts" and
hit me in the face!"

❦

KIWANIS ANNOUNCEMENT

   John Wheat, president of Reno Kiwanis Club had received
a letter requesting club assistance with an important matter.
He read the letter at one of the meetings.

John Wheat, President
Reno Kiwanis Club
C/O Holiday Inn
1000 E. Sixth Street
Reno, NV 89503

Dear Mr. Wheat,
   Allow me to introduce myself: I am the Reverend Godfrey
Daniels and I head up a traveling evangelism ministry that
was in Reno last month. I had in my employ a young man of
good family named Jacob Lindstrom who had fallen on hard
times in recent years. Jacob was far advanced down that
rocky road to perdition for a man of such tender years. He
had drunk himself into a state of indolence, sloth, low
ambition, failing health and complete social ridicule.
   At our tent meetings I would have Jacob sit near the
podium as I delivered my best sermons on the evils of drink.
He would sit there bobbing and weaving, burping and passing

141

gas as I would use him as a pathetic example of the end result of a life of consuming that devil's beverage...Whiskey!!

We have been very successful in each Nevada town visited...drawing surprisingly large crowds and converting goodly numbers of citizens in Fernley, Fallon, Austin and Eureka from lives of abject sin, debauchery and wickedness to that straight and narrow road to salvation.

Well, I am sorry to report to you that Mr. Lindstrom has died and I am heartily sorry for this event.

Mr. Wheat, I was wondering if you could recommend one of the members of the Reno Kiwanis Club as a replacement for Mr. Lindstrom for the remainder of the summer tour of southern Nevada and Arizona.

Please contact me after you have had the opportunity to present this to the members of your Kiwanis Club.

With best personal regards, I am,
Your Servant

Godfrey Daniels, D.D.

YO QUIERO TACO!

This very big man...about 425 pounds of him...sat at the bus stop at Meadowood Mall in Reno waiting for a City Fare ride to Washoe Medical Center for his clinic visit. He had a fine looking AKC Chihuahua puppy peeking out of his pocket. While he was waiting, he would take his puppy out, pet him, talk to him and return him to the warmth of his oversized pocket. The right bus came along, and as he approached the door, the driver said, "I'm sorry sir, the only animals allowed on our coaches are seeing-eye dogs!"

Our quarter-ton gentleman backed away from the bus and returned to his seat. According to the schedule on the wall, another coach should be along in about 12 minutes. He just waited and thought.

Just before the next bus arrived, our man unzipped his pants and slipped little Pancho inside. The bus came, he got on and sat back for the ride.

This lady sitting across the aisle noticed that he was squirming quite a lot and asked, "Sir, is there anything wrong?"

He responded in a low voice pointing to his fly region, "Lady, I've got a dog in my pants!"

"Well, my goodness!" exclaimed the lady. "I hope he's housebroken!"

To which the fat man grimaced, "Lady, he ain't even weaned!"

❦

IN A PICKLE

There used to be a pickle processing and distribution plant out off Fourth Street in Reno in the late fifties. They would receive large tractor trailers full of those small pickle cucumbers, dump them in brine of one kind or another and slice 'em, dice 'em, bottle 'em and ship 'em out.

Carl Smokes had been working for the company about a year when one day he came home and told his wife, "Honey, I've got this obsession and it is getting stronger every day I work at the plant."

"What is it, Carl? Can I help?" asked his concerned wife.

"I don't think you can. Maybe I need help!" Carl stared blankly out the window.

"Come on, Carl! We've always been able to talk."

"OK," said Carl, but with reservations. "I have this compulsion to stick my thing in the pickle slicer!"

"Forget it Carl! You're a damned fool to be thinking such nonsense! Put that stuff out of your mind. You can't give in to it!" was her stern advice.

Carl really took his wife's advice to heart and completely dismissed his compulsion for about two months. He came home one afternoon quite a bit before his shift ended.

"I'm sorry, honey, I know I'm weak, but today I put my thing in the pickle slicer!" Carl winced.

"You're a bigger fool than I ever thought possible, Carl. What did your boss do?"

"What do you think he did? He fired me!"

"What did they do with that pickle slicer?" quizzed his wife.

"They fired her, too!"

❧

THE RULES

Harold applied for a job at an all woman real estate office, but quit after reading the following:

The female always makes the rules. The rules are subject to change at any time without notification. No male can know all the rules. If the female suspects the male knows all the rules, she must immediately change the rules. The female is never wrong. If the female is wrong, it is due to a misunderstanding which was a direct result of something the male did or said. The male must apologize for causing the misunderstanding. The female may change her mind at any time. The male may never change his mind without the consent of the female. The female has the right to be angry or upset at any time. The male must remain calm at all times unless the female wants him to be angry or upset. The male is expected to mind-read at all times. If the female does not feel well, all rules are null and void. The female is ready when she is ready, the male must be ready at all times. Any attempt to change the rules could result in bodily harm.

DOWN THE TOILET!

A tragedy befell the Orson household that fateful day in the mid 1920's. Clyde and Susan had built a nice home on the outskirts of Sparks, Nevada and had everything completed but the bathroom. Clyde had dug a deep hole and built a temporary "one holer" until they could raise enough money to have a septic system installed.

It wasn't bad enough that they both died on the same day and it wasn't bad enough the way they died. What was really bad was the limerick that came out of this tragedy:

There once was a man named Clyde
Who fell in an outhouse and died!
He had a wife named Sue
She fell in there too!
And now they're interred side by side!

MURDER MAID TO ORDER!

The maid picked up the phone on the second ring and the voice on the other end hurriedly commanded:

"Quick, let me speak to my wife."

"I can't do that; she asked not to be disturbed!"

"This is an emergency; get her on the phone!" the man commanded again.

"I'm sorry, sir, but I have my instructions. She is not to be disturbed."

"Listen, woman, I just won the Nevada megabucks slot jackpot...twenty million dollars...and I want to tell her."

"Sir, I still can't do it," replied the maid.

"Tell me why she can't come to the phone or I'll fire you on the spot!"

With that understanding and "splainin," the maid replied, "She's in bed with her lover, that's why!"

The man was shocked! He thought for a while and came up with this plan.

"I want you to do something for me. I want you to go where I keep my gun, take it out and go into the bedroom and kill both of them. For that I will give you one million dollars...do you understand?"

"Yes sir, I think so. But how can I be sure you will pay me when I do the job?"

"You have my word. I will meet you this afternoon and give you the money."

She put the phone down, and after what seemed to be a very, very long time, the man heard two shots. A moment later the maid was on the phone.

"I did it! I did it! Now, when can we meet?"

"Hold on," replied the man. "What did you do with the gun?"

"I threw it in the swimming pool."

"Swimming pool, we don't have a swimming pool. Wait a minute, is this 555-2732?"

❧

GET A GRIP, SIR!

It wasn't exactly opening day at the northern Nevada Sperm Bank on Ryland Avenue in Reno, but it was close to it. Traffic, as you can imagine, would be sparse for a business of this type in the opening months. Owners were, however, confident they had made a safe investment.

The smartly uniformed attendant, a lady named Kim, was shuffling papers around when an elderly man entered the office and made his way to her desk.

"Yes, sir, what may I do for you?" she cheerfully asked, expecting him to ask for directions to the Senior Care Clinic down the hall.

"I'd like to make a deposit," he responded sternly.

"Are you sure you're in the right place," asked Kim, now thinking this old timer thought he was in the bank down the street.

"Lady, I know where I am and I want to make a deposit. Please don't think that just because I have gray hair and wrinkles that I don't have something to offer. I come from a long line of robust people on both sides. We have been scholars, effective elected officials, and community leaders in this country for over 200 years. Now, does this answer your question."

147

Without saying a word, Kim handed him a stack of papers to sign and a jar. After fifteen minutes, Kim began to wonder what was going on. She walked past the door and heard noises she couldn't understand. She asked, "Mr. Eggleston, are you all right?"

"Give me a few more minutes," was the response.

Another ten minutes went by and Kim had about enough. She went back to the room and with a special key opened the door. There was Mr. Eggleston sitting in the corner naked from the waist down, exhausted, sweating and looking thoroughly confused.

"Lady, I've beat it with my hand, I've twisted it, put soap on it. I've hit it on the wall. I've hit it on the table. I've run warm water over it. I still can't get the top off this jar."

PLANE LANGUAGE

On Flight 367 from Las Vegas to Reno a young Episcopalian priest was having a terrible time. The flight had been unusually bumpy. There were updrafts and down drafts, pitching and yawing and shuddering...lots of shuddering. He was praying about as hard as he could and then the pilot came on with "We'll be landing shortly at Reno-Cannon International Airport (the name of this airport would be changed as soon as Sen. Howard Cannon was voted out of office...the new name, and more fitting name, would be Reno-Tahoe International Airport). It's been a rough ride from Las Vegas; just bear with us a few more minutes. Make sure your seat belts are fastened and your tray tables are put away and your seat backs are in their original upright and locked position. Thanks for flying Hughes Air West." The worst was not over and the next eight minutes were just awful. A baby began to cry, one passenger used the barf bag and then everyone applauded with gusto when all wheels were safely on the runway.

News of this bad weather, near crash landings and calls to the newspaper from passengers who had come in on previous planes had created a media event at the airport. Two reporters and one TV news team were waiting to make a story for news at eleven and the next morning's paper.

As the shaken passengers deplaned, most avoided the news scene, others made comments. The young priest, on having a microphone shoved in his face and being asked, "How was it, Father?" made some brief, pertinent comments about this being a fear-filled time for him and about being reminded of his own mortality and how fragile life is. Before he walked away, he was asked his name and his denomination. "I am Father Charlie Stones of St. Stephen's Church here in Reno...I am an Ecopalian."

"Father," said the news lady, "you said Ecopalian, what exactly is an Ecopalian?"

As he walked away, he commented, "That's an Episcopalian with the PIS scared outta him!"

SENSE AND INSENSITIVITY

On another occasion...On *Hughes Air Worst*...make that *Hughes Air West*...Flight 366 from Reno to Las Vegas, a nicely dressed young woman carrying an infant seated herself after stowing her carry-on bag under her seat. She had no sooner gotten comfortable when she noticed the man next to her was studying her baby with some displeasure.

"Ma'am, I hope you don't take offense, and I'm afraid you will, but that is the ugliest baby I have ever seen!"

Well, that did it. Mary Killian picked up little Tommy, summoned a cabin attendant and demanded, "I want to be moved to another seat, this man has insulted me!"

"Yes, Ma'am. Come with me, I'll bring your bag in a moment." She showed the young woman to a similar seat several rows back and apologized by saying, "Ma'am, I'm very sorry that you feel you were insulted. As soon as we are airborne, I'll bring you a nice cup of coffee and a banana for your monkey."

OLD TIMERS' DISEASE

The Reno police department got a cell-phone message that a man was in some distress at the bus stop on South Virginia at Plumb Lane. A black and white was dispatched, getting there within minutes of the call. Seated on the bench was a nicely dressed man in his late sixties, possible early seventies sobbing uncontrollable.

"Sir, can I help you?" asked the patrolman.

"No, I don't think you can!" cried the older gentleman.

"There must be something I can do for you, maybe call someone to come pick you up...maybe a friend or relative?" inquired the policeman.

"I tell you, there is nothing you can do for me!" directed the senior citizen.

"Sir, if you don't let me help you, I'll have to take you to the station."

Choking back some tears and sobs, the man, introduced himself as Norman Robb, told the following story:

Norman related that he got married at twenty five to a young lady he had met in college. They lived together seven years and their drifting apart had begun shortly after their marriage. It seems she was an excellent lover, both before and after their marriage, but was a terrible cook and housekeeper. His apartment was always a mess, so much so that he could never bring anyone there or have any social contact in his home. On mutual agreement they got a swift divorce and went their separate ways.

Mr. Robb got caught up with his story and broke down crying again. The policeman patted him on the shoulder and encouraged him to continue.

Several years passed and the man got married again, this time to a beautiful woman who was a meticulous housekeeper and cook...a gourmet cook! However, their love life was a sad thing. Norman said he tried to overlook the lack of enthusiasm she showed for any and all close body contact, but it slowly and methodically destroyed their marriage. Her skills in the kitchen could not compensate for her disinterest and lackluster performance in the bedroom. They divorced but only after 25 years of marriage.

Then the tears came in earnest! The peace officer did not have the skills to calm the man down, after a few minutes of this however, Mr. Robb continued his tale.

Ten years went by and our gentleman married again. With this marriage, he got the best of all worlds. His new wife, an elegant lady he had met at St. Stephen's Church, was an excellent housekeeper, wonderful cook and knew how to make him happy in the bedroom with energy and regularity. Life was good, and he was finally a completely happy man. With that he began to cry, the tears flowed, the sobs were unceasing.

"Sir, it seems like you should be a totally happy man. You have what you always wanted in a wife, why are you so unhappy now?" asked the nonplused officer.

Norman Robb wiped away the latest flood of tears, caught his breath and said, "I can't remember where I live!"

GUIDELINES FOR LIFE

Remember the story about the little sparrow who was flying south for the winter from somewhere up north? When he got over Reno in the Truckee Meadows, his wings iced over and he was compelled to land in a horse corral south of Windy Hill.

There he was, cold, nearly frozen to death, and lifeless. A young girl had just been out to her barn feeding and watering her horse and saw this little creature shivering and dying. She picked up the sparrow and, with a stick, made a hole in a fresh pile of horse manure and placed the little fella in it.

It wasn't long before the little bird was thawed out and feeling pretty good in the warmth of the horse mess. He began to first chirp and later sing a happy song.

There was this coyote who was coming down from the hills about this time to find a bite to eat. A mouse, a rabbit, a cat, or a small dog would do nicely. He heard the singing and followed the music to its source.

He surveyed the situation and with one gulp, ate the little

sparrow feathers, feet and all.

One has to wonder if any good could ever come out of a tragic story such as this. Well, there is a strong moral...and it is this:

Someone who puts you right in the middle of a big mess is not always your enemy, and someone who takes you out of a very big mess is not always your friend, and if you are in the middle of a very big mess, keep your damned mouth shut!

❦

CONVERSATIONALISTS

These two residentially challenged...homeless people...I really mean bums...happened to meet on the corner of First and South Virginia streets in Reno. This corner had been taken over by bums in recent years with the closing of the "historic" Mapes Hotel and Woolworth's Five and Dime store. There is a certain bum-charm about this corner. It is near the parks where they, the bums, can sleep during the day. It's close to the casinos where an enterprising guy or gal can score a coin or two in the slot trays every now and then before being run off, and it's close enough to the Gospel mission and Salvation Army where hot meals can be had when it comes to that.

On this occasion, these two bums were quite drunk and they seemed to know each other. One bum said, "Sure is windy!"

"It ain't Wednesday, it's Thursday!" retorted the second bum with certainty!

To which the first bum smiled and said, "Me, too! Let's go get us a drink!"

153

LEANING IN THE RIGHT DIRECTION

A very nice couple in their late forties had been taking care of Grandpa at their Caughlin Ranch home since Grandma had passed away some two years previously.

Grandpa was in good health, but he was experiencing the first stages of memory loss, depression, anorexia and stubbornness. The "kids" tried to take care of him, but each worked and they were becoming increasingly aware they could no longer take care of him at home.

It was not easy...none of it. Grandpa did not understand, and what was going on when they took him to visit several assisted living facilities. Some were nicer than others, some were more expensive than others.

The day came when Grandpa was left at Northridge Senior Care Center after several visits with the administrators and staff. Grandpa looked as if he liked the place from the start, but who could really tell?

During the next week, Grandpa was comfortable at his new home. One thing annoyed him, however. Anytime he was sitting and started to lean over to the right, and orderly would come to straighten him up. When he was watching TV and he leaned over to the left, a nurse would come straighten him up. When he was sitting at the dining table and would lean way forward, one of the dining room staff would straighten him up. This went on everyday and evening for almost a week.

There were several calls to Grandpa during the week. These calls were non-productive. Sometimes he would not say anything. On the next Sunday after he was admitted, the couple paid a visit.

"Grandpa, what do you think of your new home?" asked the daughter-in-law.

"I don't think much of it; I don't like it!" he answered grumpily.

"What don't you like about the place, Pop?" asked the son. There was silence.

"You don't like the food?" asked the son, pressing for an answer.

"The food is good," responded his father.

"You don't like your room?" asked the daughter-in-law.

"My room is very good," was the surprising response.

"How about the other people here? Are they bothering you or anything?"

"No, they pretty much mind their own business."

"Well, Dad," asked the son, "What is it you don't like?"

The old man looked at his son sadly and said, "They won't let me fart!"

❧

A LIFE FULL OF IT

The story continues. Not about the old man who wasn't allowed to slip a little gas, but about that same nursing home. There was this local TV station in Reno that sent a reporter and cameraman out to the Northridge Senior Care Center to do several sound bites on "Secrets Of Longevity." This particular home appeared to have an edge on other facilities in that its residents factually lived longer. Maybe it was the water; maybe the diet; maybe there was an attitude there. Whatever it was, seniors lived several years longer there than in other homes in northern Nevada.

The crew was headed by Beverly Shap. The newest in an interminably long list of "Cub Reporters" Channel 24 (KNNV) had hired in its attempt to make a meaningful showing in the local news ratings. She was accompanied by a cameraman named Ernesto Caballa, an immigrant from San Salvador. Ernnie was very adept at camera, but not skilled with the King's English.

After checking in with the office, Beverly and Ernnie were lead to the recreation room and introduced to a man seated in a wheelchair in front of an oversized TV.

"Mr. Goodwin, this is Miss Shap and her friend Ernesto from the TV station to talk with you and some of the other residents. Do you have a moment or two?" Mrs. Talso asked very gently.

"I suppose so, what did you say her name was?"

"Just call me Bev, Mr. Goodwin," she directed to Ernnie to start the camera.

"We are talking with Mr. Charles Goodwin here at Northridge Senior Care Center in Reno." She shifted focus to the old gentleman and asked, "Mr. Goodwin, to what do you attribute your long and obviously healthy life?"

"Bev, I feel good all the time, I exercise, try to eat the right foods. I stay away from junk foods, fatty foods, starchy foods..." Mr. Goodwin wasn't finished when Ben interrupted, "Is there any other advice you would like to offer to younger people in our audience?" Bev asked charmingly.

"I avoid alcohol, smoking, staying up late at night, over eating, chasing painted women. I go to church regularly, try to keep a positive attitude and laugh a lot. It's worked for me...I'm 89 years old!" With a smile, he turned back toward the TV.

Sensing the interview was about over, Bev turned toward the camera and closed this portion of her interview with, "Wow, 89 years old! Thank you, Mr. Goodwin. I see a beautiful woman sitting on the couch over there. Let's go over."

Bev and Ernnie walked over to the woman and began talking to her "on camera..."

"Hi, my name is Bev from Channel 24. I understand your name is Carolyn Dankworth, and if you have a moment, I'd like to ask you some questions. Do you think that would be all right?"

The woman nodded and wiped a few cookie crumbs away from her mouth.

"You're obviously a senior citizen, Mrs. Dankworth. Why do you think you have lived so long?"

"Young lady, I've always taken care of myself. Not only my body, but my mind as well. I've always kept busy. Haven't ever touched a drop of whiskey, never smoked, no coffee, eat good food, tried not to worry about things, I like a good naughty joke every now and again, I take long walks around this place every day and I read a lot. I always get a lot of the questions right on 'Jeopardy.' On my next birthday, I'll be 100 years old, so I guess it's working!" She smiled as she looked directly into the camera.

"Gosh 100 years old! I'm going to follow your advice, Carolyn. Maybe I'll live as long as you. Thank you so much, Carolyn Dankworth.

Just then, Ernnie spied an extremely old man all shriveled up, shaking, mumbling to himself, sitting near a potted plant, gazing out a window. He nudged Bev, pointed toward the man and the two approached him.

"Sir, may we talk with you? We're from Channel 24 and

157

we're doing a piece on 'Secrets of Longevity.' We would like to get your thoughts, OK?"

"Sure, but you'll have to speak up. My hearing started leaving me last year," he said in a low voice.

Bev raised her voice to accommodate this most senior looking man, "Mrs. Talso says your name is John Knobel and you've been at the residence three years. Would you like to tell us about your lifestyle?"

"I sure would. Maybe it will help some of the young folk out there. You see, I have made it my life's work to drink as much liquor as possible every day of the year. In addition, I smoke two to three packs of cigarettes each and every day. Sometimes I have to stay up most of the night to do this smokin' and drinkin.' When you do this as much as I do, there's not much time to eat or exercise, so I rarely do either of 'em. I love the ladies here and I chase them whenever I'm up to it. Right now I have three ladies I visit on a regular basis, usually late at night. We have a good time too!" Mr. Knobel winked at Bev and she quickly determined he was not a harmless old codger!

"That is amazing, Mr. Knobel. How do you do this at your age? By the way how old are you?" asked an astonished Beverly Shap.

"Next Thursday, I'll be thirty six!"

QUESTIONS ASKED IN RENO

Does the term "tax planning for the future" suppose that one can tax plan for the past?

Isn't the expression in a song sung by Linda Ronstadt

misleading and incorrect? "The difficult I'll do right now. The impossible will take a little while." If something is impossible, it can't ever be done, right?

Are these expressions redundant? "Consensus of opinion;" "Close proximity;" and "New Beginnings?"

Could you picture this happening? "Little Harold has grown a foot since I saw him last!"

When Smokey-the-bear exclaims, "Only you can prevent forest fires!" Isn't he nothing but a trouble making liar? Do you suppose he never heard of lightening?

Don't you think the guy who invented the hand blow dryer they use in restrooms ought to have one installed in his bathroom at home?

What do you tell a couch potato husband with two black eyes? Nothing! His wife has already told him twice!

Would you believe boxer Mike Tyson in his fight with Evander Holyfield turned to referee Mills Lane and asked, "Pardon me, Mills, do you have any Gray Poupon?"

Since 'Barbie' now has a smaller figure, would you believe "Dr. Ken" is now a plastic surgeon who plans to give her a 'boob' job?

Did you hear about the haughty Virginia City woman who informed Mark Twain, "Sir, did you know that the word 'sugar' is the only word in the English Language in which 'su' is pronounced 'shu'?" Mr. Twain is reported as asking her "Madam are you sure of this issue?"

Do you think piano player and Reno entertainer "Big Tiny Little" likes to eat "Jumbo Shrimp" in the "Biggest Little City in the World?"

Do you think the drafters of the preamble to the U.S. Constitution really thought they could "...create a more perfect union?" Isn't 'perfect' an absolute?

Do you really think there can ever be a truly 'kinder, gentler' Internal Revenue Service?

Do you remember when the word gay meant happy? When being called a 'Swinger' was a very good thing? When the term 'fat and sassy' was a compliment? When no airports and no schools in the nation used metal detectors? When Russia was our enemy and Iraq was our friend?

If you remember any of these things, then you're probably very old!

THOSE NEVADA DOCTORS

THOSE NEVADA DOCTORS

Nevada doctors are as motley a bunch today as they were in the early days of the state. They came to Nevada to get away from some place else. Some came here because other state medical licensing boards were already wise and wouldn't take them. Some came here because it was perhaps the last place on the globe they could hide with the hope that all those things they hated about the places they left wouldn't catch up.

I remember a reasonably true tale about a young doctor and his bride who settled in a small mining town in central Nevada in the 1950's called Austin (or was it Eureka?). They had a booming little practice there for several years until the medical examining board got wind the good doctor was no doctor at all. The best and only credential he could muster was a first-aid class at a local fire station back in his home town. The board had no choice but to charge him with practicing medicine without a license and virtually running he and his wife out of town.

Well, the townsfolk got pissed at this! Not a doctor for hundreds of miles and some fancy board over in Reno runs these nice people out of town. Gees! These same people wrote the governor over in Carson City complaining of this intrusion and the governor sent his best sycophant to get to the bottom of it all. The conclusion was that the doctor was not qualified or authorized to practice medicine anywhere in the world and he couldn't stay there. To this the townspeople commented in a loud voice "We don't care if the doctor had a license or not. He and his wife were nice people and they provided a valuable service to our town!" Nothing more came of this, but it was probably the beginning of an orderly transition to professional medicine in the Silver State.

Most of the stories found in this next chapter were told to me by Nevada physicians. Rarely have I found a Nevada doctor without a rollicking sense of humor. Occasionally I have run across a doctor who fails to appreciate a good joke or the telling of it. I run for cover!

A GOOD IDEA AT THE TIME

A professional wrestler: I like that term, but I wonder what is the word 'professional' doing there. What is professional about a 250 pound bad tempered behemoth seemingly pounding the living hell out of another idiot. What is professional about biting, gouging, kneeing, hair pulling and verbally assaulting another 'professional'? I think nothing is. So, what makes these performances so loved and what makes these 'professionals' so admired, and what makes this whole spectacle a $22 billion per year enterprise? Go on now and figure!

One of these 'pros' called for an appointment with Dr. Eugene Spots in Reno and pleaded so sincerely, urgently, the receptionist got him in quickly.

In the doctor's examining room, the wrestler, a 29-year-old "professional" truck driver who decided to become a "professional" wrestler, told the following story:

"Dr. Spots, I am a wrestler and I go by the name 'Marco the Destroyer,' you've probably heard of me. I do mostly scientific wrestling and I hold the northern Nevada belt for defeating seven women wrestlers at the same time." During this pause, Dr. Spots responded negatively with a slight shake of his head.

"Last night, Doc, I was wrestling a man named 'Maddog Glick' whose only claim to fame is that he could break a baseball bat over his head. Anyway, we had met earlier and decided on our routine, you know, who would get beat up first, then second and then who would take the fall. I knew something was wrong when we met in the middle of the ring and he slapped me a good one right off. When we got in a clinch, I asked him what that was all about and he told me his ex-wife stole his pick-up truck and he was really pissed. I also asked him not to hurt me anymore and he agreed.

"Well, that didn't last long. He kicked me. Slapped me twice more and bit me on the arm when I had my best step-over-toe-hold on him. Finally, I told him to cut it out which only made him madder!

"After I did a fair flying face kick and a world class 'jump rope' on his throat, he got me into such a grip I never saw before. The pain was something you write home about and I could hear bones snapping and cracking. This was not in the script; it was then I realized this man was out to harm me. I was so twisted and knotted up and my vision blurred. I looked up and I saw wrestler's trunks with a set of balls hanging out. I could hear the referee counting and I did the only thing I could think to do...I took a big bite of those balls! With that my opponent flew off me, landed on his back. I fell on him and the ref counted "one, two, three...you're out!"

"Let me get this straight, Mr. Marco. You bit your opponent's testicles and you're here for treatment? I don't understand!" quizzed the doctor.

"No, doctor. They weren't his balls...they were mine!"

❦

LOVE DOESN'T ALWAYS WORK!

Dr. Robert Clarkson of Las Vegas thought he had seen a pretty good sampling of American people in his long years of practice. People who were classified as *worried well*, hypochondriacs and people who were seriously ill, but would never let their illness get the better of them. He had never seen a patient who presented with the following condition.

"Dr. Clarkson, I am being slowly driven insane and my health has been effected to the point that I either kill myself or kill my wife. She nags, complains from morning till night, spends money wildly, never listens to me, and always has an extremely negative attitude about everything. Doc, she even cuts up my steak at the dinner table. I can't stand to be around her. I don't love her, and no matter how badly I treat her, she will not give me a divorce!"

"Have you tried marriage counseling?" asked Dr. Clarkson.

"She wouldn't consider going to those people. Never...end of subject!" replied the distraught patient.

"George, don't think of killing her...ever. You will spend the rest of your life in jail. You will bring disgrace to yourself and your children and you will never forgive yourself."

"But, Doc, what can I do? We can't afford separate residences and I can't live with her...under the same roof!"

"Here's what you do, George...love her to death!"

"You're going to have to explain that, Doc."

"Beginning tonight, start a program that goes something like this: first thing in the morning, make love to her. Before you leave for work, make love to her again. Mid morning come home and jump in the sack. Take an extended lunch hour and make love to her. During the afternoon, drop by the house and make love to your wife. Before diner, and after dinner do it. When you two go to bed at night, really put your heart into it. Repeat this program every day, George, and in three weeks, on the outside, she will be dead; you will be free of her and you won't do time! Do you think you can handle this?"

"Why don't I just kill her outright, doc...have you seen my wife?" the patient asked.

"Never mind...just do it!" directed the physician. "Give me a call in a couple of weeks and give me a progress report."

Two weeks went by and Dr. Clarkson had not heard from the patient so he stopped by his home one afternoon. After ringing the bell, George greeted him and directed him back to the patio area. George painfully eased himself into his chaise and took a big gulp of fortified orange juice. He looked awful...cadaverous in fact! His cheeks were sunken, eyes had dark circles, he'd lost weight, and obviously was drinking heavily! His wife was puttering around in their little garden. She was radiant! Her hair was perfect, complexion rosy and she was humming and singing, the absolute picture of health and happiness!

"Tell me how it's going," quizzed the good doctor in a low voice.

"Doctor, I've done just as you suggested. Morning, noon and night, especially at night, I've made love to my wife and it has just about killed me. There's only one thing that keeps me going, Doc."

"What's that, George?" asked Dr. Clarkson.

"Just knowing that in one week," responded the husband, "she dies!"

ॐ

SMALL COMPARISONS

Elizabeth had been seeing a young man for some time, but her father—a cardiac physician—did not think it was really serious. He didn't particularly like the guy anyway.

As it turned out, however, the two *were* serious and on a Saturday night, the man came to pick up Elizabeth for a movie and asked if he could speak with Dr. Williams privately.

The two went into the large living room and the young man began:

"Dr. Williams, Elizabeth and I have been seeing each other for almost a year and we love each other. I would like to ask you for her hand in marriage!"

The doctor was floored! He could not think of anything to say, but he had to come up with something quick! He didn't think this was a good match and he had to give this guy a good reason to bolt.

"Son, I appreciate your interest in my daughter, but I think it is only fair to tell you that Elizabeth has acute angina," said

Dr. Williams in a very solemn tone of voice. The young man thought a moment and said, "That's great, Doctor, because her tits ain't much!"

ॐ

TWENTY YEARS B.V. (BEFORE VIAGRA)

In Las Vegas holistic medicine abounds. What it is exactly no one knows, but it is supposed to be the answer to high priced conventional medicine. One doctor I know said that holistic medical care is the equivalent of giving medicines with no proven value to people with no proven illnesses. If this is true, and it sounds like it just might be, then anything a holistic practitioner prescribes will work!

A true story about this holistic hocus goes something like this. A man who frequently visited his urologist because of recurring impotence asked, "Doc, I've been here half a dozen times and you are not helping me one bit. If you can't help me, then refer me to someone who can."

When the man left the office, he had a slip of paper on which was the name of a man named 'Tamarence' who was a holistic health practitioner in North Las Vegas.

Our patient, let's call him Harold, went directly to the office of Dr. Don Tamarence, and after an hour's wait, a ten minute interview and a two minute physical exam, was told, "I think I can fix your problem. Here is a compound that has been approved in Romania and parts of Chad known to work in cases such as yours. This is powerful healing. You only use it once a year. After taking this powder with a full glass of water, you say 'One, two, three!' You will be cured of your impotence problem for as long as you wish."

"Gee, Doc, that's great! But tell me, how do I get, you know, back to 'normal' afterwards?" asked an amazed Harold.

"All you do then is say 'one, two, three, four' and it will return to it's former state. But remember, you will not be able to use this potion for another year, do you understand what I'm saying?" Harold nodded, paid his bill and went home.

That same night, before retiring, Harold took his potion and decided to surprise his wife with the good news. He gets in bed and as his wife slips under the covers, Harold shouts gleefully, "One, two, three!" And with that, Harold experiences an immediate, profound and magnificent erection!

His wife turns to him and says, "Harold, what did you say 'one, two, three' for?"

❦

STAND UP FOR DOCTORS

"Good evening, ladies and gentlemen, welcome to the umpteenth annual holiday party of the Washoe County Medical Society. I say umpteenth because few in this room really know how many we've held over the life of this organization. My name is Wayne Harper, your president.

"I was told by a lady who knows these things that years ago the auxiliary to the Medical Society, then called 'The Doctor's Wives'...*a politically incorrect title* as it was later determined...had a social meeting and each of the twenty-five or so women present was asked to stand, introduce themselves, and tell a little something about themselves. This one woman, new to the group, had recently married a local doctor who made it his life's work to marry as many women in the world as possible. She stood and said, 'I am Helen Turnbull, the most current wife of Doctor William Turnbull!' "I always thought that showed class and a good sense of humor! I am your most current president, I'm happy and proud to be that!

"Tonight, we are going to have some fun. This has not been a fun year, a year in which doctors have had lots of laughs. This year the legislature beat us up again as usual, HMOs continued to get between us and our patients, Bill Clinton persists as president of the U.S. and Harold Burnside persists as President of Washoe Hospital Center. It's been that kind of year.

"With us tonight, however, is Phil Mundo, a stand up comedian from Las Vegas who is building quite a reputation for his knowledge of medicine and the medical profession. Phil flew in from Vegas this morning, and boy, are his arms tired! Please welcome Phil Mundo!"

"Thank you, current president Harper, Reno audiences are the best in the world!! Gee, it's great to be in 'The Biggest Little City in the World.' Whatever that means. It's an oxymoron, huh? Like legal ethics, like jumbo shrimp, like organized medicine!

"I've been appearing nightly at the beautiful 'Desert Inn' showroom. One night there was this big noise, I learned they were imploding the entire building. They don't tell people anything in Vegas! On the way to the hospital, I complained about not having much room in the ambulance. They stopped and made four lawyers get out!

"I guess you heard my son is a doctor. He had a tough time with all those tests you people have to take, and I'm not sure he did all that well on them.

"He thought 'labor pains' meant getting hurt on the job. Yeh, he answered 'a punctuation mark' to the question 'what's a coma?' He thought a band-aid was a musician's assistant! He thought the common duct was the mallard. He thought 'lumbar puncture' was a hole in a 2 by 4. He answered, 'the consequences of frostbite' when asked, 'what is lactose?' He said 'the study of roadmaps,' when they asked him what Pathology was! 'Inpatient?' he answered, 'where is the scalpel?' When asked why human feces was tapered, responded, 'so your butt doesn't slam shut!'

"He told a patient in the recovery room he had some good news and some bad news. The patient asked, 'What's the bad news, Doc?' 'While you were under, an Orthopedist with wife trouble cut off both your feet by mistake!' After the patient calmed down, he asked, 'What could be the good news after that?' My son responded, 'The patient in 32-B wants to buy your Nikes.'

"He had a part-time job helping Dr. Burt Duddman do circumcisions at the hospital. Did he make good money? No, but he got a lot of tips!

"My son, the curious doctor, had some questions for the medical examining board when they were finished with him, he asked, 'Why do all doctors in research have British accents? When a doctor tells a guy to quit smoking, the guy doesn't tell his wife...when he tells him to go on a diet, he doesn't tell his wife...but why is it when the doctor tells this guy he needs more sex, he runs home and tells his wife???'

"My son called me and told me the following true story:

"There was this sheik from a wealthy middle eastern principality called 'Olay'...remember their world-famous export 'Oil of Olay'? Oh, never mind! This sheik and 29 of his most beloved and newest brides came to Reno to visit that

172

famous fertility clinic, 'Babies-R-Us.' The sheik wanted a large family fast!

"After the collection and distribution of the necessary ingredients, the entourage went back to Olay after paying a truly enormous bill to Washoe Hospital Center. Within nine months (nine and one half on the outside) his wives produced twenty single-birth babies, six sets of twins, one set of triplets, two sets of quads and from the last report on CNN, all the kids and moms were doing fine.

"Time passed and on the day his triplet sons came of age, the sheik, whose royal name was 'Yah Bouteh'...yeh, 'Sheik Yah Bouteh'...called them for their coming-of-age-wish-granting, a tradition in Olay. 'Congratulations my sons, as you know, on your twenty first birthday you may have anything in the world you want. Anything except a Chia plant. I hate Chia plants!' He grimaced. The young men thought for a brief moment. Finally the eldest (by one minute) said, 'Thanks, oh magnificent father figure! I have been thinking about this moment for many years. All my life I have taken my pleasure in tinkering with little gasoline engines and motors. I like to work on them and hear them putter and sputter. This is my special interest.' With that, the sheik waived his arms to his accountants and said in a loud voice, 'Mohammed, go out from here and buy my son the General Motors Corporation!'

"The second oldest son stepped forward and said, 'Oh gracious and benevolent pappy, my desires are similar to those of my older brother. My special interest is in tinkering with batteries and little electric motors and making sparks and stuff, to which the father shouted, 'Abdul, my trusted financial assistant!' The Harvard trained CPA rushed to the sheik's side, 'I command you to go out and buy the General

Electric Corporation for my son!'

"The third and last born of the trio was in deep thought, finally stepping forward and saying, 'Oh, all knowing big daddy, my desires are not like my older siblings. I desire nothing on such a grand scale as you have provided them. My desires are quite simple. All I have ever wanted in this life was a Mickey Mouse outfit!' 'Kareen Awheet,' commanded the dad, 'oh valued keeper of my accounts, depart immediately to Reno, Nevada, and buy *Washoe Hospital Center!*'

"Back here in Reno, I learned today that St. Mary's Hospital staff has been successful in the first total arm transplant in the state. A young woman had recently died and donated her body to science. The recipient was a UNR student who had lost his arm after passing out and falling under a moving truck at the last football game tailgate party.

"Chief of staff at the hospital, 'Skeet' Holcomb commented that the surgery went flawlessly and the patient was expected to have a complete and uneventful recovery. (Skeet was told to say that by the hospital attorney.) My son, the doctor, talked with the patient about three weeks after surgery and learned that almost everything was fine. The patient had one concern however. 'Doctor, my right limb will always be smaller than my left and that's OK because it's a girl's hand and arm. It will never be as strong either, I know and fully accept this. My problem is, that whenever I go to the bathroom, it won't let go!"

"St. Mary's, or as it is known in some circles 'Our Lady of Interstate 80,' using the same team of crack surgeons, announced today the attempt to re-attach the hand of a UNR football player was a failure. It seems that the micro surgery

174

went quite well, everything looked fine, but sadly, the boy's penis rejected it!

"Dr. Tom Bradley, respected Reno urologic surgeon told me the other day that he got a call one evening from one of his patients who said, 'Doc, at 5:30 each morning, I get this urgency and I urinate for what seems to be four or five minutes!' 'Mr. Jenson, that's a good sign and it's quite normal,' said Tom. 'But, Doc, I don't get up until 7:30!'

"Doc Bradley also told me that towards the end of a busy day at his office he asked his nurse to go see if there were any more patients in the waiting room. She came back and said, 'There's a man out there with one kidney named Gordon who needs to see you.' Dr. Bradley directed her, 'Well, go back out there and find out the name of his other kidney and *send him in!*'

"The story got around about a doctor in Sparks who was exhibiting anti-social insensitive behavior. The Board of Medical Examiners was notified and they referred the physician to the County Medical Society's 'Impaired Physician' committee for evaluation.

"The complaint went something like this: the wife of a patient undergoing major surgery was waiting anxiously for news from the doctor. Unfortunately the patient died on the table and then it was the physician's sad duty to inform the patient's wife. Our insensitive medic went to the public address system and announced, 'Will the widow Thompson come to station 'B' and pick up a death certificate.'

"The medical examining board asked the young doctor if he couldn't have been more tactful. He responded, "I thought about lining up all the women in the waiting room and saying, 'All you women who have living husbands, one step forward. Not so fast Mrs. Thompson!' That probably would have been better, don't you think?"

"The medical examining board unanimously agreed and dismissed the charges.

"Then there was Dr. Jack Brothers who knowing he might not ever make a fortune in his medical practice, tried his hand at inventions. He had some successes, but also had several near-miss failures.

"One invention was a capsule you place in the toilet tank to color and freshen water in the bowl. He came close to having a certain winner, but chose the wrong color...he chose 'yellow.' His wife, Yvonne, wanted 'red!'

"His next attempt was a disaster. He invented an ejection seat for a helicopter. The trouble started after the first trial run. Try as he may, he couldn't get anymore Washoe Medical Center administrators to be test pilots.

"His last attempt was developing a new and excitingly different mouthwash which would remove tartar and plaque, strengthen gums, whiten teeth and last all day. All his research went perfectly, but when the new mouthwash reached the market, it bombed! Dr. Brothers couldn't understand why 'Garlic Fresh' didn't make it!

"Dr. Brothers once had a job counseling students and parents at the UNR School of Medicine. One day he called in Mr. and Mrs. Smallwood telling them he had good and bad news about their freshman med student son. 'It's come to my attention that your son, Robert Smallwood, is hopelessly homosexual. That's the bad news...the good news is that he was just elected 'Queen of the May!'

"Dr. Donald Moldman, the famed Reno psychiatrist reported to the State Psychiatric Society the following case history about a woman who presented with bad dreams...nightmares, if you will.

"'One night, Doctor, I dream I am a wigwam. All night long, I'm this wigwam!' exclaimed the distraught women.
"Yes, go on," replied the psychiatrist.
"The next night, I'm a tee pee. Yes, that's right. I'm a tee pee all night long! What's wrong with me, doctor?"
"Relax, Mrs. Linguini, you're just two tents!"
"How about that new drug for men called 'Viagra!' It works too well, I've heard. Like the Reno doctor's wife who over the years had gotten used to her husband's impotence. In fact, she rather enjoyed it! Now that he is taking Viagra, he just worries the hell outta her all the time with his continual sexual advances. My new word for what his wife is experiencing is "Viagravation!"
"Gosh, folks, I could go just like this for several more minutes, but I see by the old clock on the wall, and the hook Dr. Harper is hiding behind his back, that my time is gone. You've been a super audience and I love being with you. Remember: A doctor who treats himself and his family has idiots for patients. And my very last piece of advice to all you doctors out there is "Never treat a disease not covered by a national health organization!"

"Thank you. You're a funny man and we enjoyed your humor. You can be certain we'll have you back. Oh, by the way, when your son finishes his training, tell him to look some place else to practice. We already have too many doctors who think they are comedians practicing here!"
Good night everyone!"

❧

A LITTLE CONSIDERATION, PLEASE

Harold was called at work by Dr. Rex Baggage's nurse and was asked to come by the office when he got off work. The doctor wanted to talk with him about the tests he had recently taken.

"Rex, what is it? What do the tests say?" Harold asked nervously.

"Harold, this is the worst news I've ever had to tell one of my patients. Remember the last time you were in and I examined you for quite a long time? Well, the tests I had you take showed you have the rarest form of anatypmenologetically-symtolaryncaronattessik-sumatonoloponoty. This is the most serious and deadly form of what I just said on the planet. There is no cure, and as best I can determine, you have just a few short hours to live! By morning you will be dead; I'm sorry to have to tell you this, but I have consulted with doctors in as far away as Tonopah and Elko and they concur that my diagnosis is correct. I wish there was more I could tell you. Please make your account current on your way out and good luck!"

Well, that just about did him in right there in the doctor's office, but he did manage to get home and tell his wife. They decided to spend their last night together having a wonderful meal, watching their favorite video and retiring early to enjoy their last intimate contact before he departed.

They made love three, no, four times before 12:00 and a couple of times after 2:00 a.m.. Harold shook his wife tenderly at 4:00 a.m. for some more romance to which she replied, "Sorry, Harold, some of us have to get up in the morning!"

❦

A HOUSE AIN'T A HOME

They were a newly married Montana couple, Terry and Martin, and their dream of a happy life included a ranch. They saved their money for a year and a half, but soon came to realize that by the time they could buy the ranch of their dreams, both would be on social security. After some discussion and much agony, they decided to move to Carson City and look into the possibilities of entering the "ranching" (whoring) business there. When they came into town, the first visit they made was the 'Kitty Ranch' on the outskirts of Carson City in Storey County. They talked to the Madam and informed her of their dreams. She told them it might take as long as eighteen months of flat-on-her-back vigorous work to earn enough money for the sizable down payment on the real ranch they wanted in Montana. She also told Terry to go to a doctor in town for a complete physical checkup and extensive bloodwork.

Not all doctors in Carson City took care of working girls, but one physician thought it was an honorable thing to see to their needs. Dr. Robert Brownlee was called, an appointment was made, and a thorough exam was made of Terry, inside and out. A large amount of blood was taken for study. A week later, Dr. Brownlee's office called and asked the couple to come in for a consultation.

Dr. Brownlee asked, "Are both of you sure you want to do this? It seems like a very severe way to accumulate enough money to make your dreams come true, don't you think?"

"Doc, I hope you can see this from our point of view. Terry loves me and I love her. Nothing she will do out at the

Kitty Ranch can change that. We also want you to know there is no other way to make this kind of money as fast. How were the tests?" asked Martin.

"Oh, they're fine. I knew they would be. Here is your certificate, and please, Martin, come see me if you have problems with this decision...I'll be glad to help anyway I can." And on that the couple departed.

It wasn't a month before Martin was back in Dr. Brownlee's office with a very concerned look on his face. "Doc, remember you asked me if I ever had problems with Terry becoming a whore to come see you? Well, I got problems!" Martin almost broke into tears.

"It's OK, Martin, tell me about it," directed the kindly middle aged family practitioner.

Martin collected himself and said, "It was OK for the first two weeks, Doc. But I got awfully lonely and one night I decided to go out to visit my wife."

He broke down crying. After pulling himself together he said, "I told the woman I was married to Terry...one of the girls...and wanted to be with her awhile. And do you know what, Doc? They charged me $65.00!"

LITTLE THINGS MEAN A LOT

It was somewhat of an unusual situation for Dr. Wesley Halsey, a very fine general surgeon in Reno. He had been practicing in "The Biggest Little City in the World" for a number of years, and he, like many other people in Reno, did not understand what that expression meant. Anyway, Dr. Halsey could appreciate a joke or a story better than most doctors on the planet and could tell them without equal.

He tells the story about one of his patients, a man named Jeremiah Gish, who came into his office telling the receptionist he had a personal problem that he only wanted to discuss with the doctor. He visited with Mr. Gish for a good ten minutes before asking him what he could do for him.

"Doctor, I want you to take a look at this," Mr. Gish said somewhat embarrassed. With that, he took down his pants and underwear and revealed what Dr. Halsey later described as the smallest penis he had ever seen. It was barely one half inch long.

"Mr. Gish, that's the damndest thing I have ever seen!" exclaimed the doctor.

"Yeh, Doc, it's been swollen like that for over a month!"

FAINT OF HEART

Dr. Halsey, around a campfire at the annual "Pure In Heart" bowhunt for deer, has been known to tell the following story about the Pope and his physicians.

The Pope's heart was failing rapidly. His doctors were convinced the end was very near unless there was a complete heart transplant. Assembled physicians were increasingly alarmed that the Pope had few remaining options.

The Pope was informed of this by his trusted assistant Father Antonito who suggested that donor arrangements be made as quickly as possible due to the Holy Father's delicate condition.

At the time of this event, there were simply no hearts immediately available. There were long waiting lists and the

Father refused to consider preferential treatment. Time was short and one physician, a righteous man named Florentino Americus, suggested to Fr. Antonito that word go out announcing the Holy Father would accept a heart from one of the faithful. What an honor this would be to donate your heart to the Pope! This seemed like a good idea and the word went out.

Days passed and no one came forward. Not one person was willing to make such a supreme sacrifice! What a set-back!

Plan "B" was put into effect. This simple plan, a joint venture between Fr. Antonito and Dr. Americus, consisted of having the Pope, on his next good day, address the multitude in St. Peter's square and for him to outline what now would be the organ donor selection process. A feather would be liberated over the people and at whose feet the feather landed, that person would be brought forward for the donation. A true act of providential selection!

The Pope rallied the very next day and was strong enough to deliver a magnificent homily from that little balcony overlooking the huge square. He ended with a statement of his condition and the method of allowing the Almighty to select the person to give the Holy Father many more years of life on earth. The feather was blown over the masses and the Pope and his supporters went back inside to await the results.

Fr. Antonito was convinced the plan would work. But as they waited, he noticed the strong smell of Garlic wafting in from the open doors. He got up and went to the balcony and to his amazement and disappointment, the feather had not fallen at all; there were fifty thousand followers blowing as hard as they could to keep it aloft!

❦

THE WRONG QUESTION

This story reminded the good doctor of one more of his favorite Pope stories. This one he told with feeling!

A janitor in the heart of Dublin, Ireland was ready to retire after serving as sexton of the third largest Catholic Church in the City. He had cleaned and repaired the church, dug the graves and rung the bells for forty years and it was time to move over for a younger man to have this honor.

The congregation was well aware of Mr. O'Tool and his retirement plans and had collected a surprisingly large sum to assist him with his meager retirement. Even more funds were collected to provide this dedicated servant with a trip to Rome and an audience with the Pope!

The trip through "The Chunnel" was thrilling as was his train ride through France and over the Alps, through northern Italy and into Rome itself. He visited all the sights of Rome, toured the Vatican City and the big day finally came. Mr. O'Tool was ushered into a rather large room with many beautiful paintings and Frescos adorning the high walls. At the end of the room was an ornate door. As Mr. O'Tool was standing there in awe of everything...a truly humble man...the door opened and in came two robed men wearing red hats followed by the Bishop of Rome...the Pope himself! Immediately, the Irishman fell to the floor, his face flat on the marble with his arms extended. He lay there quietly praying as the Pope approached.

"You may get up and stand before me," gently instructed the Pope.

"Oh, no, Your Grace! I could never stand before your

Holy Radiance, the Holy Father, the Pope of Rome!" said O'Tool, groveling as he spoke.

"Yes, my child, you may arise and tell me something about yourself."

"Faith and begora! I'll be thanking you the rest of me life for allowing me to be in your presence, Holy Father. Sure and it's difficult for me to believe that me, a lowly church janitor for forty years, is allowed to stand before your holiness!" said the janitor rising reverently.

"From your accent, my son, I can tell you are from Ireland. Is that true?" asked the Pope.

"Oh, yes, Your Imminence. I was born a true son of the Emerald Island and I will die in Ireland a happy and blessed man for seeing the glow from your holy face!" Mr. O'Tool almost shouted.

"Tell me, my son, are you from **Northern** Ireland?" asked the Pope.

With that, Mr. O'Tool's demeanor changed. He became agitated, shook his fist at the Pope and shouted, "You'll be keepin' a civil tongue in your head, you ignorant Bastard!"

CHILD'S EYES

Dr. Halsey tells quite a few stories that relate to where he grew up...Hushpuckinah, Mississippi. Yep, that's right, Hushpuckinah! It took me a long time to learn to pronounce it, too.

He tells one story I like in particular about the preacher who would come to Hushpuckinah on a year-round schedule to baptize the locals. After a brief baptismal program in nearby Alligator, Mississippi he hit Hushpuckinah in early January. While the river wasn't frozen it was damned close to icing over. The minister, after giving a fine sermon about Baptism, set about his immersion duties, taking the children first. This one little girl was all dressed up in her finery and was lead somewhat reluctantly by her mother into the cool river.

"And now I baptize you in the name of the Father, the Son, and the Holy Ghost!" Exclaimed the preacher as he held his hand over the mouth and nose of the little girl and dipped her below the water. She came up with a gush of water as the minister shouted, "Amen and Amen!"

The next candidate was a little boy smartly dressed, wide-eyed and obviously scared to death. The minister took him under and brought him back with a flurry. The boy was lead back up to the riverbank covered with a blanket after being toweled off pretty well.

The last child to receive the baptism was a heavyset little guy, who was equally scared. The minister cupped his hand over his face and dipped him below the surface. By this time the preacher's hands had suffered the severe chill of the river and he lost his grip on the chubby little fella. He searched around with his hand, grabbed a handful of hair and reorganized him to where most of the worshipers on the shore did not notice anything out of the ordinary had happened.

When the fat little boy came out of the water he commenced to shouting, "I have seen the Lord! I have seen the Lord! I have seen the Lord!" He was lead back to the shore still proclaiming as they dried him off, covered him with a blanket and lead him to where the other two children were seated shivering. He again shouted, "I have seen the Lord!"

One of the kids asked, "Was he kind of mean-looking and had big eyes?"

"Yeh, that's right! Did you see the Lord, too?"

"I seen something like that, but I thought it was a bull frog!"

❦

WOOD? MY EYE

Harry Lane did not do everything right when he tried to refasten the screen door spring. First he should not have been on eye level with it, second he should have had completely dry hands and thirdly, he should have had a better grip on the spring when it slipped out of his hand and popped him in his right eye.

The next day, after emergency surgery, he left the hospital heavily bandaged over part of his head and right side of his face. The spring had so severely damaged his eye that it had to be removed. As time passed, healing occurred and Harry had become accustomed to wearing his eye patch, but anticipated getting a glass eye as soon as the doctor gave the OK.

On his next visit to Dr. Tam Konky's Reno office, he broached the subject. "Doc, when can I get a glass eye and how much do they cost?"

"Mr Lane, I would say that any day now you would be an excellent candidate for a prosthetic eye. As to what they cost, I can only say that the very fine replacements are quite expensive...running into several thousands of dollars." He jokingly added that he had a friend who could whittle him an excellent eye out of wood for under $50.00.

"Gosh, Doc!" exclaimed Harry, "I didn't know they cost that much. Tell me more about your friend who whittles."

"He has done several for my patients, enjoys doing it an actually produces a very fine eye. He whittles it to my specifications and paints it up to look very much like your other eye and you have to admit, the price is quite reasonable."

They sealed the deal. Harry got the specs he needed and he went directly to the eyeball man. It was a most pleasant encounter. Harry paid the man and in three days picked up and installed his new eye.

At first, and for several days, Harry had some difficulty in keeping the eye focused straight ahead. Then he learned some maneuvers to match the movement of his good eye. He practiced for hours in front of his bathroom mirror.

In three weeks he was ready to publicly try his new orb. He went to a very low bar on Lake Street in Reno one evening and sat at the end of a rather long bar sipping a genuine draft. The evening went by slowly and nothing happened. Then something happened. In the dim light, Harry could see a rather attractive figure of a woman make her way to the other end of the bar. He had the barkeep send her a drink with his compliments. This went on for about an hour then the band started playing. This was Harry's moment, he went to where she was seated and asked the lady if she would like to dance. Just then he noticed that an attractive figure was all this woman had going for her. She was so very ugly. Her most prominent feature, her nose, was the size of a large banana! No one ever asked her to dance before, no one! In her exuberance to accept his offer she shouted out, "Would I! Would I!"

To that, Harry, hurt and embarrassed, shouted back, "Big nose! Big nose!"

DOC, IT HURTS WHEN I DO THIS...

It wasn't long before the nurse receptionist came into Dr. Halsey's office saying, "Your favorite hypochondriac is here to see you, Doctor. Shall I send her back?"

After nodding approval, Dr. Halsey thumbed through his memory about Rita Schmidt. Yes! He remembered her well; she was the one most likely to have a tombstone with the inscription, "There, I told you I was sick!"

In she came and out came a list of symptoms only heard by medical students at the University of Nevada School of Medicine at exam time!

"Miss Rita, what is your chief complaint at the moment?" asked the 'concerned' doctor.

"Dr. Halsey, I don't know where to begin. Whenever I touch my head there is such awful pain! Whenever I touch my knee, there is excruciating pain! Whenever I touch my stomach, such pain you'll never know!" As Rita touched those places, the doctor could tell she was, indeed, having the pain she described.

After a brief examination, Dr. Halsey assured her, "I have found the cause of your pain, Mrs. Schmidt, you have a broken finger!"

INITIAL DIAGNOSIS

It was a trying time for all doctors in the Reno area. Many older physicians didn't let a day go by wherein they didn't think of 'hanging it up,' quitting medicine. Patients were constantly telling them what to prescribe due to direct advertising on TV by pharmacy houses. Health maintenance organizations usually had a local doctor (who had already 'hung it up') telling them what, where and when doctors could take care of their patients.

This one doctor, a man named Thornton, felt sure he had coined a new expression about managed cared. When asked what he thought of health maintenance organizations he commented, "The initials 'HMO' looks like 'HOMO' and that means 'queer medicine!'"

One night he was home relaxing after a busy day at the office and later at the hospital when his wife shouted, "Hey! Thornton! Come in the bathroom quick!"

As he approached the bathroom, he was met with wet feet and a very distinctive odor. When he peered in he could see the toilet overflowing! He automatically reached down and turned the water supply off via those two knobs behind the bowl. Next he got out his 'friend' the plumber and commenced to pumping away. He'd pump awhile, open the valves again, flush the danged thing only to have it overflow again. Finally in desperation, he went in the den, looked up the closest plumber and called for help.

Within twenty minutes, the doorbell rang and there stood a very attractive woman in her early thirties who greeted the doctor with,"My name is Elizabeth Wainwright and you called a plumber?"

He guided her back to the bathroom where she started the

'snake' process leading to the clean 'flush' of an unclogged drain. It took no more than fifteen minutes.

She met the doctor in the living room and began working on a bill. When finished, she handed Dr. Thornton a bill for $125.00. The doctor was speechless, almost.

"My gosh, woman I'm a doctor and I don't get this much for my services!"

After taking his check and collecting her tools of the trade, she walked to the door as she said, "I know, I used to be a doctor!"

❦

SHE'S OK...HE'S NOT!

Dr. Kavelski had always been receptive to taking a few minutes to hear his patients' concerns, even if they were not relevant to their immediate problems. The doctor was an Otorhynolaryngologist. That's an ear, nose and throat specialist. There was a time when residency programs trained these kinds of doctors with one more specialty added: eyes. Yes, and EENT was a ophthalotorhynolaryngologist. As you can see, this moniker won't fit on those brass shingles doctors hang outside their offices so 'eyes' spun off to another specialty to prevent this. This is a true story.

Anyway, Dr. Kalvelski was seeing one of his Reno patients on which he had done some minor surgery recently and asked, "How are things going, Mr. Garrett? Your surgery went well."

"I'm fine, Doctor, but I think my wife is losing her hearing. I talk to her and she doesn't even respond most of the time." Hearing this, Dr. Kalvelski said, "Mr. Garrett, it's not uncommon for people your age to lose a good bit of their hearing. Here is a simple test you can do. If she doesn't pass it, have her come in and I will check her out. Stand about twenty feet from her and ask a question in a normal tone of voice. If she doesn't respond, move about ten feet closer and ask her again. If she still doesn't answer you, try five feet. If she still has not heard you call for an appointment."

Mr. Garrett went home and later that evening he moved across the living room from the kitchen where his wife was working, and in a normal tone of voice asked, "Honey, what's for dinner?"

There was no response. Garrett moved to about ten feet and asked, "Honey, what's for dinner?" No response!

He then moved to within five feet and just before he quizzed her for the third time, she said, "Before you ask me that again, Wayne, I've already told you twice, we're having Ham and Beans!"

❦

BE CAREFUL WHAT YOU SAY!

It is not certain that John Sandestadt told the following story, but he might have!

On a cold winter's night very near Two Harbors, Minnesota, a traveling salesman with car trouble went to the closest farm house to find lodging for the night. After knocking at the door and waiting quite a long time in the bitter cold, the lady of the house opened the door. She had been in the back of the house finishing up the dishes and was carrying a huge frying pan.

The salesman was astounded at the size of this

scandahoovian woman and could only say, "My God, lady, you're big enough to play with the Green Bay Packers!"

With that, she gave him a good smack with the skillet, shouting, "I don't play with nobody's packer but Oly's!"

❦

A QUARTET OF STORIES

Ron Slaughter, a tenured pathologist at Columbia Sundown Hospital on Maryland Parkway in Las Vegas has a quartet of stories in his extensive repertoire. Each is a real hoot! The first of his magnificent four goes like this:

THE MORE THINGS CHANGE

Several years after the Russian Revolution, two weary men are trudging through the heavy snow in Moscow. One man has a slightly aging fine wool coat and a beautiful ermine hat with flaps. The small man with him is dressed warmly, but his clothes are old, torn and dirty. The smaller man speaks:

"Uri, isn't it vonderful! Before the revolution vee could not be valkink together like dis, you being a nobleman and me a lowly peasant! It is truly vonderful now!"

The other man does not speak. Later the two men go into a bar and have several drinks of vodka. The little man speaks, "Uri, is dis not vonderful? Before the revolution vee could not be drinkink like dis together, you being a nobleman and me such a lowly peasant!"

Again, the nobleman does not speak. As they walk through the heavy snow, the several drinks began to take effect and they move off the road onto a snow field and began to relieve themselves. The little Russian starts in again, "URI, dis is most vonderful, I vill remember dis all my life! Before the revolution vee could not be pissink in the snow together like dis, you a nobleman and me a lowly peasant, but tell me, Uri, why is it that I am making tracks in the snow and you are not making the tracks?"

Uri, the former nobleman finally speaks with utter contempt, "Eet ees because, Boris, I am pissink on your coat, you lowly peasant!"

❦

DELIBERATE IN ALL THINGS

This next tale must be told by someone skilled in rolling their 'Rs' as Scotsmen and Dr. Slaughter do.

On the outskirts of Edinburgh, Scotland, a regiment of the famed Highland Guard has been camped for several weeks. A sergeant has been dispatched by his captain to go into town on an important mission. He enters a store and addresses the proprietor, "A fortnight ago, I visited your establishment and made a purchase. It is my duty to inform you that the product you sold has failed to perform as warranted!"

The chemist, as they call them in Scotland, made a cursory apology and asked what kind of product was purchased and what was wrong with it.

"The product purchased was a rubber; the problem is that it leaks," replied the sergeant.

"Sir, what is it you'll be wanting me to do about that?" inquired the store owner.

"I have been instructed to learn how much it will cost to have the product replaced and how much to have it repaired!"

said the officer without a hint of humor.

The chemist comes back with, "Sir, to have the product replaced will be a threepence and to have the product repaired will be a tuppence!"

The sergeant turned quickly and left with the comment, "I shall be back on the morrow with a decision."

At dusk the next day the sergeant returned, went up to the counter and addressed the owner. "Sir, the regiment has voted to have the rubber repaired!"

IT'S NOT THE SIZE OF THE DOG IN THE FIGHT!

O'Dool staggers into the Shamrock Pub in the heart of Dublin and as he approaches the bar orders a large whiskey. The barmaid knows this man and asks as she pours his order, "What in the world has become of you, O'Dool? You look as if you've had almost all the hell kicked outta ya!"

"It's that I been fightin' with that low down, dirty O'Tool; for over half an hour we been fightin'!" was his reply.

"Why, O'Dool, you're twice the size of O'Tool!"

"Yes, but he had a crowbar in his hand!" answered the battered Irishman.

"And just what was it you had in your hand, might I ask?" quizzed the barmaid.

O'Dool saluted the bar maid and took a big drink of his whiskey.

"Mrs. O'Tool's ass!" he replied. "While it's a fine thing to behold, it's not worth much in a fight!"

194

THE THRILL OF VICTORY

A Norweigian athlete at the Olympics in Atlanta was working out in one of the gyms when asked by an official, "Pardon me, are you a pole-vaulter?" The athlete curtly replied, "I am not a pole, I am a Norweigian and my name is not valter!"

🐨

WORDING IS EVERYTHING!

"Doctor, my life is a mess! I have a lot of trouble falling to sleep, when I do, I wake up at three AM and can never get back to sleep. I'm drinking too much and it's just possible that I might get fired because I'm tired all the time!" Thus was recited the litany of all his depressed patients, thought Dr. Stan Roberts.

Stan knew his patients could live better chemically. He knew Elavil and Prozac were wonder drugs of the century...right up there next to aspirin. These drugs allowed depressed people to function quite well and to begin enjoying life anew. The doctor didn't always prescribe these drugs right away. Sometimes there were alternative approaches.

Frederick York, a middle-aged man who, when he was not worrying about his messed up life, was a postman in Fallon, Nevada. He was the archetypal depressed patient. The above comments were his actual words on March 29th when he presented at the office nearly in tears. Dr. Roberts gave him a cursory examination to rule out any major conditions or illnesses then invited him into his office for a chat.

"Mr. York, you appear to be a healthy 45 year old man, but

I know you are not feeling well and you're certainly not happy. I'm not going to prescribe medication at this time, but here is what I am going to prescribe. I want you to plan to have healthy meals, I want you to stop drinking for a month, I want you to buy a treadmill and begin the exercise program I'll give you. I also want you to develop some better sleeptime habits. Your bed is for making love or for sleeping. It's not for eating, watching TV or reading long novels. Do you understand what I'm saying?" instructed the doctor.

Mr. York shook his head in agreement, although he would have much preferred the drugs!

"And one more thing, Frederick, do what I do. When I feel down, I go home to my wife at noon or in the early afternoon and make love to her. It always picks me up and then I'm fine." Try all the things I've suggested and see me in a month." Stan grinned as he related this advice to the man.

It was almost exactly a month when Mr. York came back to see Dr. Roberts.

"Well, how's it going, Frederick? You look well and happy!" Stan asserted. Frederick York responded energetically, "Doc, I have never been better. I'm eating the right kind of food, sleeping great, lost a little weight and, by the way, you have a nice home!"

MEDICAL TERMINOLOGY

Dr. Tom Bradley and his urologic surgery associates were among the first in Northern Nevada to perform male sterilization procedures. They were not immediately accepted by the male population in northern Nevada, but the female population thought they were just super! The idea caught on and this group has done a ton of them over the years.

It was Dr. Bradley who may well have coined a new expression. When one of his still unconvinced patients asked if the procedure would change his sexual performance, Dr. Bradley reassured him, "There won't be a vas deferens!"

Here's two stories told by a doctor mentioned earlier:

STICK TO YOUR DIAGNOSIS!

John Sandestadt and Naomi had come to Reno years earlier from Minnesota. John was a dentist who decided to become a medical doctor and he and Naomi had moved to Reno to finish out his military obligation at the Veteran's Administration Hospital. Soon as that tour of duty was over, John opened his medical practice in Reno. John had been highly trained in medical diagnosis with the accent on being certain the first time around. A doctor who constantly changes his mind on diagnosing patients soon would be without patients.

One of his very first patients was a rancher from Smith Valley named Douglas Anderson. Douglas presented with abdominal symptoms, and after exam and history, Dr. Sandestadt said, "Mr. Douglas, my examination reveals that you have locked bowels."

"Locked bowels? What in hell are you saying, Doc? I've had diarrhea for three weeks now!" exploded the rancher.

"My diagnosis stands...you have locked bowels...locked in the open position!"

❦

DON'T PLAY IT AGAIN, OLY!

Dr. Sandestadt is famous for telling this Christmas story each Yuletide season to a handful of close friends. It has become a tradition. It goes something like this:

On a cold winter's evening in the northernmost part of Minnesota...near Two Harbors, I think, residents were celebrating the season with a feast...lots of Ludafisk and gallons of Aquavit. A band played all the favorite tunes and there was dancing and story telling. Sven had set his sights on Inga and had danced almost every dance with her.

When it was time to end the evening, Sven asked permission to walk Inga home. When they got to Inga's door, it was just a matter of smooth talking...then he was inside. Next thing you know he was in bed with Inga and they were having a fine time.

"Oh, mine Got," yelled Inga. "That crunching you're hearing belongs to Oly's boots making straight for home. He vas not expected until tomorrow. Qvick, you have to hide!"

Sven looked around the small cottage and there was *no place to hide*.

"Qvick, up in the rafters and cover yourself with something!" directed Inga. Sven climbed up in the overhead space, covered himself as best he could with an old quilt, but, sorry to say, his testicle hung down through the rafters.

Oly came through the door and after greeting Inga sensed something was wrong.

"Vat iss going on here...something iss going on!" he shouted.

"Iss nothing going on!" snapped Inga.

Just then Oly looked up and pointed to something he was not very sure of. He, too, had consumed quite a lot of Aquavit and his vision was blurred. "Vat is dat?"

"Vat is vat," delayed Inga.

"Dat, vich is hanging down?" pursued Oly.

"Oh, iss Christmas bells. I hung dem up just for you."

"Christmas bells?" and with that Oly grabbed an ax handle in the corner of the room and took a mighty swat at the "bells."

"Vat iss dis, the bells do not make the yingle, yingle!"

Just as Oly reared back to give another, even mightier swat, Sven who was already in horrible pain exclaimed in a very loud voice "Ye...sus Christ. Yingle! Yingle!"

SCOPE THAT OUT!

It wasn't long before Dr. Sandestadt had built quite a reputation for himself. He became the doctor to which doctors sent their families. Quite an honor then and now.

One day a patient named Stash Kavelovich came to him with an unusual chief complaint.

"Doctor, I'm embarrassed to tell you what is happening to me. Promise you won't laugh?"

John nodded curiously.

"It started about a week ago. I got a bad case of gas and every time I would pass a little, it would go 'Honda!... Honda!'" Stash laughed a little...which matched John's chuckle.

After disrobing and hopping up on the examining table, John produced this long chrome rod and after explaining what he was going to do with it, proceeded to do what he said he was going to do with it.

He looked around quite a bit with the proctoscope and said, "Aha, there it is!"

"What is it, Doc?" asked Stash expecting the absolute worst.

"Mr. Kavelovich, you have an abscess in your descending colon and I will give you some anti-biotics which should heal it in about a week."

"But, Doc, what about that strange noise when I break wind?" asked Stash as he began putting on his clothes.

"That will go away in about a week too. It has been my experience that..." John paused and smiled a little.

"Abcess makes the fart go 'Honda'!"

THAT NEVADA LEGISLATURE

THAT NEVADA LEGISLATURE

Nevada state senators think they are better than assembly people. They are elected every four years rather than every other year and swear on the Bible and the Book of Mormon they are more deliberative, pensive and better serve the public because they do this.

The Senate meets in smaller chambers since only 21 seats are needed. Normally, deliberations can be quieter than that raucous, less dignified bunch down the hall.

Some Senators go on to higher office, although I can't imagine why they would even want to. No Senator I ever heard of ever aspired to be elected to the Assembly, but the converse is usually the rule.

In Nevada the gaming industry hires all the heavy hitting lobbyists and thus gets about everything it wants and nothing it doesn't want. Every year, for example, some assembly person introduces a bill to initiate a state lottery and every year that piece of legislation is unceremoniously killed. The gaming industry does not welcome a state lottery because it just might eat into hefty revenues, though I don't see how. One year the industry gave us an alternative...it is called megabucks. Just drop some quarters in certain strategically placed slots and win millions! Some people do!

A few years ago when the move to ban smoking in public places was passing in other states, a bill was introduced in our legislature to ban puffing in grocery stores. Now that makes sense, doesn't it? The bill was passed with one minor amendment: the area around the checkout stands...the place where the slot machines and their devotees hang out...was exempt from the law. It probably won't be long before checkers and assistant managers file suits like the airline cabin attendants have done saying second hand smoke is wrecking their health! I like the idea of dropping my change in and occasionally winning a few dollars. The only smokers I see in those areas are seniors hired to make change.

The legislators meet every odd numbered year in mid to late January and get salary and expenses for 60 days then expenses only are paid for the remainder of the session. Sessions used to go to early July. Starting in 1999 they have to stop at the end of May. Someone figured it up; during a two year term of office, an assembly person will earn about fifteen thousand bucks total.

I think it was 'Big Daddy' Unruh the longtime speaker of the California assembly who coined this caveat to new (male) legislators I saw in a lobbyist's office a few years ago:

"If you can't eat their food, drink their liquor, screw their women and look them right in the eye while voting "No" on their bills, you don't belong here!"

Lots of new legislators find it hard to vote that way after enjoying the four items mentioned earlier. Many tenured legislators do it all the time.

An interesting thing happened to me on the way to the forum, eh, Nevada legislature...before coming out here, I was a three session lobbyist from the South Carolina legislature. That body met on Tuesday, Wednesday and Thursday six months of each year. Since most solons were lawyers, this allowed them to have most of the week to go back home and practice law. I was astonished that Nevada had open legislative hearings. The South Carolina Senate and House of Representatives did not allow committee meetings to be open to the public. When a hearing came up on a bill on which the people represented wished to provide testimony, we would wait on the twenty foot long mahogany benches outside the hearing chambers. Sitting near us would be representatives opposed to our views on that particular bill. There were long silences on that bench and then this huge door would open, the committee secretary would call proponents of the measure in to give their testimony. Afterwards they would be excused and the opponents would be called in. It was strange, but then, what did I know...that was the way it was done! This was the first venture into the lobbying arena for me and I just assumed this was the way it was done all over the country. Coming to Nevada legislature was like I had died and gone to Heaven! You could actually sit there and hear first hand what your opponents were saying about you and the people you represented!

State legislatures have been the brunt of wisecracks and innuendo down through the centuries. There was one quote I really liked (and I will try to find out who said it) that goes something like this.

"No man's life, liberty or property is safe as long as the legislature is in session!" Maybe it was a conservative Republican!

While we're quoting or misquoting, I'm reminded what Mark Twain was supposed to have said about the Nevada legislature while he was spending time as a reporter for the "Territorial Enterprise" in Virginia City.

When asked what he thought about a legislature that met for sixty days every two years, said something to the effect

205

that,

"...I think it should be the other way around...!"

Though not referring to the Nevada legislature, Twain could have been thinking of it when he was quoted as saying, "Members of Congress are the only native American criminal element."

❦

DEAD HEAD

The prognosis was not very good. The doctor told the patient that he would be dead within two weeks if something wasn't done about the brain disease he had. It would appear that his brain could and probably would explode by the end of the next week and there was only one possible cure. The patient, a man named Sam, would have to have a brain transplant!

"Where can I get a brain on such short notice?" cried Sam in despair.

"It just so happens that there are three brains available at the Washoe Medical Transplant Center. One is the brain of a nuclear physicist who recently died of a heart attack. The second is the brain of an astrophysicist who succumbed to an auto accident and the third brain is that of a Nevada State Senator who died of far advanced liver disease...these are available at this time and I would advise you to take one of them."

"Well, Doctor, what do you have to pay for a brain these days?" queried the man.

"They are not inexpensive, but look at it this way, if you don't get a brain, you will surely die. The nuclear physicist's brain is twenty-five thousand dollars. The astrophysicist's brain is thirty-five thousand and the Senator's brain is fifty thousand dollars," replied the apologetic doctor.

After a moment in thought, Sam inquired, "Doctor, I can understand why the brains of the two physicists are so expensive, but why is the Nevada Senator's brain the most costly of them all?"

"Well, you see it's like this, Sam. The Senator's brain has never been used!"

❦

TWENTY WELL-SPENT

One long-time Nevada legislator, William Bagacio of Reno, maintains a highly developed sense of humor in everything he does and that includes being Senate Majority Leader.

Bill enjoys welcoming new lobbyists to the legislature and usually sets an early time for a meeting or luncheon. Sometime during that get-together the Senator will learn what there is to know about the lobbyists and the legislative goals of the group or groups they represent.

Bill will take out his wallet, peer into it and exclaim he must be losing his mind! He then will, in a very sheepish way, ask the lobbyist if he could borrow twenty dollars. He will give a convincing and time proven reason for needing the money. Of course he will pay the lobbyist back the next day!

No lobbyist in his right mind would refuse this!

During the next floor session, the Majority Leader will, by name, officially welcome the new lobbyist into the "Bagacio $20.00 Club," the senate and all the lobbyists in the gallery then would give the new member a big horse laugh! Some think the Senator gives the money back or turns it over to snack bar fund or some such third party. Others think he just keeps it!

❧

THEY RARELY GO THERE

This was a story that circulated in the legislature during a recent session: the occasion was the passing of Pope John Paul. He was welcomed into Heaven ceremoniously and bypassed all those people waiting to get in. The greeting committee consisted of St. Peter, the angels and archangels and all the company of Heaven! After an extensive survey of Heaven, the Pope asked St. Peter to take him to his home-for-all-eternity which the head gatekeeper was obliged to do.

What a very nice place! A very adequate bungalow in a beautiful grassy Meadow surrounded by trees, a flowing stream and in the back was a small, but well maintained garden with shrubs and trimmed hedges. The house itself was furnished modestly, but quite comfortably. The Pope was obviously pleased. His personal dwellings on Earth were never this nice.

The Heavenly entourage toured the mini-estate winding up in the back yard; the Pope looked up and on one of the hills in the distance was what could only be described as a palace the likes of a Taj Mahal!

"Peter, would you be so kind as to tell me who lives in that splendid home on that distant hill? Could it be one of my predecessors?"

"Oh, no your Grace, that home belongs to an American

state senator from Nevada who came to us recently!" responded St. Peter.

"Allow me to get this straight, Peter. I am the Pope, the Bishop of Rome, I am the latest in a distinguished line of descendants stretching two thousand years back to the early followers of the Master himself, and I get this nice little cottage to live in for eternity. Are you with me on this, Peter? So, I get here and look on a hill and you tell me the palace I see belongs to a state senator from Nevada! Now Peter, really just how is this possible?" The Pope sounded annoyed.

"Well, it's like this Father, we get every Pope there ever was or ever will be, but this is the first and probably the last Nevada state senator we will ever get!"

❦

OPEN HOUSE

During one of the session, maybe '93 or '95, a tour was set up for a legislative field trip to view first-hand one of Nevada's commercial industries. There aren't that many industries in the state, but the list is growing and is impressive. This is usually done in the opening weeks of the session when there is time to do such things.

The legislative staff had collected names of those wanting to attend and had arranged for several buses for transport.

On the day of the tour, it was announced buses would leave from the Fifth Street side of the legislative building. The tour would take about three hours from start to finish. One of the assemblymen asked, "Mr. Speaker, where is it we are going?"

"Our tour today will be one of Nevada's legal and tax

paying industries, the Mustang Ranch Brothel east of Reno!" replied the speaker.

After the jokes and laughter subsided, it was agreed the tour would be postponed indefinitely.

❦

SAGE SAYINGS

Here are some curious quotes from people in and around the legislative halls and from our esteemed representatives within the Washington Beltway. Some are unattributed, but true nonetheless.

"Nevadan's object to turning our state into a nuclear suppository!"

"Yes, I do accept the appointment by President Bush to the post of Ambassador to the Bahamas. They have excellent golf courses there!"

When asked to explain the difference between overt action and covert action, responded, "Overt action is secretive, behind the scenes activity; covert action is out in the open conspicuous action."

Chic Hecht, former U.S. Senator from Nevada

"A smart female lobbyist has it over a smart male lobbyist because the plumbing is different!"

Anon.

"Mr. Chairman, the Nevada Sheep Ranchers' Association has asked me to tell you they are tired of the guilt trip being placed on them by the U.S. Government. It's not true...'Smoky the Bear says only ewe can prevent Forest Fires' it's a heavy burden!"

Anon.

"Mr. Speaker, everyone here knows the value of swimming programs in our elementary schools. It won't take much funding at all...teaching swimming is easy and fast. My father taught me to swim...it was a snap! Getting out of that bag was the hard part!"

Anon.

"Mr. Speaker, I rise to thank the Jewish Members of our legislative staff who have volunteered to cover the Christian Staff members who wish to be away from the legislative building to observe Easter religious services. It would be a good idea to get a list of all Jews on the staff so we could do something for them!"

Anon.

"Mr. Speaker, as a member of the minority party in this chamber and knowing the measure before us has the full support of the majority party, I want to tell my colleagues of the majority I know what a midget feels like, 'The last to feel the rain and the first to go in a flood!'"

Anon.

"Mr. Chairman and members of the Senate Judiciary Committee, this is truly an ugly piece of proposed legislation before you today. It looks like it fell out of an ugly tree and hit every branch on the way down!"

Anon.

"Mr. President, I sense this body is about to pass one of the worst pieces of legislation ever to disgrace the statutes of Nevada. This legislation will make me ashamed to be a Nevadan, it will make me physically sick to my stomach and possibly to my death. Every man, woman and child in the Silver State for years to come will remember this day '...a day that will live in infamy...!' Oh, I'm sorry, Mr. President, I thought we were discussing SB 368, please strike my comments on the bill to name the State Insect which is before you!"

Anon.

When asked by a delegation from a visiting African nation why there weren't very many black people in the area, one senator responded, "Northern Nevada winters are too cold for them!"

"If there had been an 11th commandment, there never would have been a Nevada legislature."

Argeepee

212

GOVERNOR LIGHT

The Lt. Governor of Nevada has few official duties. The Constitution obligates him or her to ascend to the governor's office and mansion if the incumbent drops dead, quits, goes to jail, or gets elected to the U.S. Senate. He is also commanded to preside over the Nevada Senate and vote only in case of a tie. A tie happens about as often as a closed casino in Reno reopens! Some say the Lt. Governor is over paid and under worked. The $15,000 salary would be spent better if the 'Governor Light' would just stay home!

One such group that thinks the Lt. Governor should stay home is the Nevada Senate. A trifling effort was made a few years ago to have the position abolished in the constitution. There wasn't even enough interest in the Lt. Gov. or the position to do this. The legislature took the bull by the horns and gave the position a whopping pay raise. All the way up to $50,000 per year. Way to go Solons!

A HORRIBLE WAY TO GO!

It just so happened that a very well known lobbyist was approached by one of the "connected" people in Las Vegas and informed that he would be paid handsomely to get a certain bill passed by the 1991 legislature.

At first the lobbyist was reluctant to accept the assignment, but said he would give it his best shot. And that he did, but the legislature was not interested in making it easier to get names removed from the "Black Book." Undesirables have their names placed in the "book" when they have violated

213

certain gaming control board and gaming commission rules and regs...those so listed are prohibited from gaming or entering casinos in Nevada.

After the session the lobbyist reported with regret, he was unable to effect passage of the measure. The man said, "We're not playing games here sir! We asked you to do a job for us and you failed! You will be punished by death or you will be made to listen to two hours of Governor Bob Miller's speeches. Which do you want?"

The lobbyist naturally picked the latter...listening to the speeches.

Early in the 1993 session, the lobbyist got a call with the same offer. "Do what you have to do to get the bill passed!"

Again, try as he may, the bill failed.

The "family member" contacted the lobbyist immediately after the session and said, "You have disappointed us again and your punishment will be death or listening to **four hours** of Governor Bob Miller's speeches!

And again, the lobbyist chose the speeches!

As expected, the lobbyist received a call on the opening day of the 1995 session with the same deal, and knowing he had no choice, went forward with his very best effort to get the bill passed. He tried different strategies: new persuasive arguments, hand-outs and testimonials. The bill faired less well than in previous sessions. As expected he got a call from a very irate Las Vegan.

"You have not comprehended the gravity of this situation. You have been given an honorable assignment on three occasions and you have failed all three times. Your punishment will be death.

"You will be taken to a place far from here and you will be forced to listen to Governor Miller's speeches until you die!"

❦

MARVELOUS MARVIN

What a breath of fresh air; Marvin Sedgewick being elected to the Nevada legislature! He was a Las Vegan, an optometrist, a millionaire and a Jew. He hit the legislature on fire, driving up to Carson City in his Rolls Royce, and did not stop until he was too ill to do just about anything. He died in 1993.

While he was with us he made his mark. A gifted legislator...and Marvin was one of my trusted friends in the legislature. Always happy, always smiling, always offered a bit of humor for anyone who would listen. And he had a wisdom that few ever possess in those legislative halls.

He loved stories about the Jewish people and had quite a repertoire. Two of my favorites were:

Moses comes down from the mountain carrying these two huge stone tablets and addresses the multitude assembled. Holding the tablets in his outstretched hands, he calms the crowd and proclaims, "After long negotiations with the Lord, Oh Children of Israel, I got Him down from twenty commandments to only ten."

There was much applause and cheering which was abruptly halted when Moses raised his hands again and spoke, "But **adultery** is still in there!"

❦

Moses later confided in one of his valued assistants that the Lord was a very tough negotiator. He figured he had done the best he could against the Creator.

After the third day of listening to the Lord God's plan for the Children of Israel, Moses asked, "Now, let me get this straight. If I hear you correctly, you're giving all the oil-rich lands to the Arabs and you're going to cut off the ends of our 'what'?"

❦

Marvin would take delight in tripping up his Bible conscious fellow legislators with the following quiz:

"Senator, refresh my memory. How many of each species of animal did Moses take on the ark?"

Whoever he asked this important question would always answer "two."

Then Marvin would say, "You're some Biblical scholar, Moses didn't have the ark, Noah had the ark!"

❦

KNOW AND CARE

Lt. Governor Stanton P. Archebald gaveled the Senate to order on opening day, and after some hoopla, prayers and introductions, was permitted a few moments to address the upper chamber. Some call it the House of Lords as opposed to that unruly group down the hall, the House of Commons.

He began, "Ladies and gentlemen of the senate, I am pleased to be here today to do my part in beginning what I feel will be the most productive session in Nevada's history. In my campaign for election to this most important post I became concerned with two moods I found prevalent in the

Silver State. One mood is that of 'ignorance' about the needs of the fastest growing state in our union. The other mood I detected is that of 'apathy' about the tremendous efforts it will take by everyone to keep our state prosperous and ready to meet the challenges of the new millennium. So, in your deliberations the next several months, be ever mindful of the question. 'What do we do about ignorance and apathy in our state?'" A few people actually applauded as the Lt. Governor turned the agenda over to the Senate Pro Tempore.

Thank you, Mr. Archebald, for those thought-provoking comments. "What do we do about the ignorance and apathy prevalent in our state?" I speak for no one but myself when I say, "I don't know and I don't care!"

❦

FIGURES DON'T LIE

Mothers Against Drunk Drivers (MADD) is a potent force in any state legislature. Mothers who have lost loved ones in accidents caused by people driving under the influence give testimony that is truly compelling. How can anyone who is right-thinking vote against them?

Like most social legislation enacted in California, Nevadans, even though they hate to do it, many times enact the same laws here. Case in point: the California legislature recently passed a law (at the insistence of MADD) to lower the percentage of alcohol in the blood from .100% to .080% when determining "driving under the influence."

The gaming industry in Nevada was opposed to it from the get-go! So the bill didn't stand a snow ball's chance on the Vegas Strip in July of passing the first time around. This is the way MADD works...never giving up! They will be back again and again until they wear legislators down to where they would reinstate prohibition just to get rid of them!

During the committee debate testimony in favor of the bill was impressive. One testifier, assigned the dull task of supplying statistics supportive of passage reported, "And Mr. Chairman, in Nevada it can be shown that 41% of all fatal highway accidents involve drunk drivers..."

To that an assemblyman, from Ely, interjected, "Ma'am, do I understand your testimony correctly? Are you saying that 41% of fatal highway accidents in our state involved drivers who are drunk? If that's correct, then 59% of Nevada's highway fatalities involve people who are cold sober; and, if that's the case, it's safer in Nevada to drive drunk!"

With that the legislator excused himself and left the hearing room. The bill never got out of committee.

60 MOMENTS

During the 1977 session of the Nevada legislature, there was increasing concern by physicians about escalating malpractice insurance premiums. In some instances premiums were doubling, tripling and in some specialities increasing fivefold over the previous year. Nevada doctors, through their state and county medical societies, were very active in lobbying the legislature to promote passage of "Tort Reform." Hopes were to reduce losses incurred by insurance companies in fighting "frivolous" cases. Thus stabilized, premiums would stop increasing so dramatically.

Somehow word of this legislative fight...doctors versus

lawyers...got back to the "60 Minutes" TV show people and a producer (there are many) came to Reno to do a little groundwork for a possible segment. After a brief evening of gathering background information, the frontman agreed to go forward. Correspondent Mike Wallace would be assigned to interview County Medical Society president, Jack Talsma, MD.

The big night came and Dr. Talsma and the CEO of the State Medical Association...the chief lobbyist...met in the executive offices of Washoe Medical Center in Reno. Mike Wallace had a previous assignment and had been replaced by correspondent Morley Safer. Mr. Safer had been briefed quite well and was aware of the situation, terminology, the players and the pros and cons on both sides of the issue.

It is very interesting the way this interview was conducted. Mr. Safer and Dr. Talsma sat and chatted for half an hour or so. The producer quietly wrote down every question asked by the correspondent. When he felt there was enough material for this portion of a ten to twelve minute TV segment, he called a halt and reviewed the questions selected with correspondent Safer. The camera was then redirected to Mr. Safer and the producer read off the question. Morley would then put the questions into his own words. The interview was over for Dr. Talsma, as the next ten minutes were devoted to carefully phrasing the ten or so questions. Dr. Talsma's answers to those questions would be dubbed in later...high theater!

During the interview, Morley Safer had been hearing a lot about lawyers filing lawsuits without merit in hopes of getting settlements for their clients from "deep pocket" insurance companies, rich doctors and hospitals. Mr. Safer asked the questions, "Dr. Talsma, don't you think lawyers have principles?"

"Yes, they do indeed," replied Jack Talsma. He then opened his wallet, pulled out several dollars and said, "They have principles and here they are!"

That question and that answer did not wind up on the cutting room floor where it probably belonged!

❦

A GOOD IDEA AT THE TIME

Several years ago certain members of the Nevada legislature got the bright idea to designate a portion of Nye County...the second largest county in the United States...as a nuclear waste depository. Legislators were told by seemingly knowledgeable people that, if this were done, untold millions of dollars could be collected every year from the federal government and no money needed to be expended.

What an idea! Simply form another county...that would then make 18 in Nevada...have certain legislators designated as county commissioners since no one lived in the proposed area and then watch the money pour in. The idea was as 'hot' as the area under consideration!

The legislature passed the bill but later had to call a special session to repeal it since its passage was so totally rejected by Nevadans.

The following is a verse written in memory of that failed thinking!

BULLFROG COUNTY

The nation needs a big old place
To store its hot nuclear waste!
A place that should be safe from quakes
From ground that moves and often shakes.
Safe and far from the nosy crowd.
Curious masses not allowed!

Out in the desert there exist
A desolate place such as this.
It's found in the County of Nye
Safe from the world's most searching eye.
It is there we could safely store
Atomic waste for evermore.

Carson solons quickly decreed
'There's an overpowering need
For a hole in a hill in Nye
Form a new county and thereby
Receive billions paid us in cash
As it is filled with fed's 'hot' stash!"

The county was right quickly named
For an old mine and no one blamed
Nevada..."Being realistic"
By looking at the statistic
Showing the cash we would accrue
National recognition too!

'Bullfrog county' thus created!
A county with no purpose stated

Except to dig out all that rough
And bury spent atomic stuff
Power plants' nuclear juices
Warheads with no further uses.

Nevadans, yet to have their say,
'Transport spillage along the way?
Earthquake! Damages could be great!
'Bullfrog county'..."Give it the gate!"
Parents, liberals all rebelled.
Solons repealed it as compelled.

Weak ideas sometimes advance.
"In favor? Aye! This is our chance!"
Hasty schemes...be allowed to die
Without thoughts of 'Give it a try!'
'Bullfrog County' was such a plan.
The people spoke; it could not stand!

Argeepee

HERE IS MY UNALTERABLE STANCE!

"And with that, my fellow Nevadans, I conclude my remarks to you tonight and thank you for the opportunity to tell you where I stand on the important issues of the day, and ask for your support in the November election, Mr. Chairman?"

The Chairman of the 'Legislator's Night' Committee approached the podium and addressed the Henderson Palisades Homeowners' Association. He asked the 45 members present if there were questions. A tall thin man in the back of the audience stood up raising his hand. On being recognized, asked, "Senator Clark, thank you for coming out tonight and giving us a fairly good picture of your positions on various issues. Could you take a few minutes to tell us your views on alcohol?" With that he sat down, the crowd cleared its throat and shuffled its feet.

"I am so thankful this question has come up and I prepared to give you my unequivocal and long-held position." The Senator paused, looked squarely at the audience and commenced.

"Sir, if you are talking about the beverage that causes our jails to be full of drunks and our hospitals to be full of injured and our graves to be filled with victims and if you are referring to that foul beverage that cause men to abandon their families and lead lives of wickedness and debauchery, and if that to which you refer is sometimes called the 'Devil's Brew' causing fist fights at our ball games, fist fights in our bars, cross, harsh words, threats and curses uttered to loving family members, the substance that causes financial burden and shame on being arrested under its influence, and sir, if you are asking my views on the liquor that causes our citizens to wager away their paychecks on games of chance thus taking food out of the mouths of hungry babes, then kind sir, I am firmly, totally and unalterably against it and opposed to it!

"But, my good man, if you are referring to that hearty liquid, that oil of conversation, which brings good friends together over a spirited cup of good cheer, and if you are referring to that uplifting, healthful drink or two each night by the hearth that has never failed to lighten the burdens of our working men and women, and if that to which you refer is the delicious beverages we drink at birthdays, weddings and

223

special holidays causing warm feelings of goodwill toward all, and if you are referring to that bottled consumable the taxes on which fills the coffers of the state treasury which then goes directly to building schools, providing hot meals for underprivileged children, that assist in providing shelter for the poor and worthy homeless, that pays for the construction and maintenance of our highways, pays tuition for college students and training for medical doctors and nurses and finally, sir, if you are asking about the whiskey and liquor that is legally sold in thousands of bars, grocery stores, casinos and hotels in Nevada's tourism and entertainment establishments that create jobs and paychecks for 400,00 Nevadans, of this liquor, whiskey, wine and beer, I am totally supportive and will fight with my last ounce of energy for the growth and expansion of its consumption, and that, sir, is the progressive stand I have chosen to take."

LADY, MY CONCERNS AIN'T YOUR CONCERNS!

The big push by the Nevada Sheep Ranchers' Association was to get some legislation to control coyotes. It seems that every few years the coyotes over breed and produce a bumper crop of sheep loving offspring. In normal years the number of sheep taken by hungry coyotes was at some sort of acceptable level, but the last couple of years the 'take,' especially among the lambs was unusually high and the sheep ranchers wanted something done about it. They wanted an extensive program to legally kill pups and adults in unprecedented numbers.

This might sound like a suitable way to handle this

224

problem, but there was this lady from the Sierra Club who had heard the ranchers were going to make a play of this kind and she was dispatched to prevent it. After introducing herself and handing out some literature to committee members, she began.

"Coyotes have been in this country since before man arrived here and we are the intruders, not them. Sheep are not native to these parts and coyotes will do what they have to do in order to survive. That may mean killing an occasional sheep! It's not an easy existence out there. Mr. Chairman and members of the Natural Resources Committee, I have given each of you an outline of the program the State of Idaho has initiated recently on the coyote predation problem. The wildlife division there has started what looks like it will be a successful effort. To begin with, Idaho has initiated a plan to capture and sterilize male coyotes..."

With that, one of the sheep ranchers listening in the back of the small hearing room jumped up and shouted in an irritated tone, "Listen here, Lady, we ain't concerned about them damned coyotes screwing our sheep, we're concerned about 'em eatin' 'em!"

GONE BUT NOT FORGOTTEN

One of the legislators, a freshman assemblyman from Las Vegas was petitioned by some group...mortuary special interest, maybe...to put a law on the books to make it illegal for living people to have any kind of sexual activity with non-living people. One could argue either side of this issue, but probably couldn't do it with a straight face.

The bill was drafted, introduced and referred to the Human Resources Committee for hearings. The only person to show up for the hearing was the author...the freshman assemblyman from Las Vegas...he encouraged the committee to go ahead and pass the bill since there was no Nevada statute covering this matter. The committee quickly moved a "do pass" and sent the bill back to the floor of the Assembly.

The speaker of the Assembly at that time was a republican form Elko whose pledge was to shorten the interminably long sessions. This would require no wasting of time on bills such as this. When this bill on 'necrophilia' was reported back to the full assembly, the speaker called a short recess and addressed the 25 member republican caucus in general and the introducer of the bill in particular.

"Fellow republicans, how in the world are we going to shorten these sessions if we keep getting bills like this one our distinguished colleague from Las Vegas has submitted? This bill has already progressed through committee and I see no other recourse but to pass it over to the Senate, but please...no more time consuming bills of this kind...OK? If there is another low priority bill to hit the floor, I will give it my personal touch, does everybody understand?" There was agreement among caucus members and just before the group was dismissed to return to chambers, the speaker said, "...it should be illegal to have sex with a dead person, this might have prevented me from marrying my first wife!"

❦

PARK AT YOUR OWN RISK!

There was ample debate on Bill AB338 'a bill to mandate the allotment of parking places in all areas of public accommodation for persons with certain physical impairments and disabilities and other matters pertaining thereto.' This handicapped parking bill was not well received due to the inherent nature of Nevada politicians rarely passing legislation to benefit special interest groups unless they are lawyers.

When the bill reached the floor after extensive testimony in committee hearings, one legislator...a man from Fallon, Nevada presented his testimony against the bill in the form of numerous questions.

"Why, Mr. Speaker, do handicapped people need special treatment under the law? Why do they need special favors doled out through the legislature? Why should a man or woman with a cane be allowed favoritism in parking their cars? Why should these parking places be so close to the front doors of these establishments...couldn't an area for handicapped people be set aside elsewhere?" The Assemblyman sat down.

The chambers were quiet for a split second, but a small distinct voice could be heard coming from the gallery where the lobbyist usually sit. A lobbyist, formerly from California where this law came from said,

"If it weren't for handicapped parking, I'd never find a parking space!"

227

DON'T MAKE ME GO THERE!

The lady of the house was busy cooking breakfast when he came down the stairs and started in, "I don't want to go there today! It's not the fun it used to be, there are so many rules! Nobody likes me, everybody asks a lot of questions I can't answer. There's an awful lot of money I'm accountable for. Everybody wants something! Everybody is mad at everybody else! Why can't I stay home today?"

The lady turned to him and said, "You just can't, that's why. You're the Speaker of the Assembly. It's Monday and you have to go to Carson City.

❧

BAD NEWS AND GOOD NEWS

There are lots of lawyers in state legislatures. They love it there...they can argue legal points, make laws, feather their own nests to a fair-thee-well! Occasionally there is a good joke that goes around the legislature at the speed of light. The following is a story told by a non lawyer at the end of a bitter partisan discussion in the Assembly Judiciary Committee:

The legal secretary picked up the phone on the second ring with, "Law offices, how may I direct your call?"

"I need to speak with Thomas Mason, please," requested the caller.

"I'm sorry, Mr. Mason is on vacation and will not be back in the office until Monday. Is there someone else who may help you, or would you like to speak with his voice mail?" The secretary had this down pat after several calls.

"No thank you. I'll call back on Monday."

228

Come Monday morning and the caller requested Mr. Mason.

"Oh, I'm sorry, haven't you heard? While on his skiing holiday, Mr. Mason ran into a tree and was killed instantly..." Before she could go through the drill about someone else helping the man, he replied,

"Oh, I see." Then a long pause and, "Thank you."

Half an hour later the phone rang again,

"Mr. Mason please."

"Sir, Mr. Mason has been killed in a skiing accident. May I direct you to another attorney?"

"No thank you," was the caller's response.

Yes, another hour passes and the caller asks.

"Mr. Mason, please."

She instantly recognized his voice and responded.

"Sir, Mr. Mason is no longer with the firm, why do you keep calling and asking for him?"

"I guess I'm just one of those guys who can't get enough of good news!"

OFFICIAL LOBBYIST TEST

To become a lobbyist in the Nevada legislature and thereby get to wear that annoying little badge, you will have to answer many, many (not all, natch!) of the following legal, moral, ethical and dumb questions correctly. Your answers will be judged by an ersatz 'Don Rickles' type comedian.

1. Is it legal for a legislator in Esmiralda County, Nevada to marry his widow's sister?

Answer: What kind of stupid answer did you give, you

hockey puck? Is it legal for a man in some dinky little back water county in Nevada to marry his window's sister? Why hell, no! That would mean, you imbecile, the man is dead!

2. A Basque sheepherder in Elko County had 17 sheep. All but nine died. How many sheep did the man have left?

Answer: If all the sheep this poor slob had died except nine, then it would follow, you mental dwarf, he would have nine left!

3. A lobbyist representing Nye County was asked to divide 50 by ½, then add 20. What's the right answer?

Answer: Maybe you can't remember that far back, bird brain, but when you divide a number by a fraction, you turn the fraction upside down and multiply. Don't ask my why, all right! The answer is 120.

4. Go to the legislative snack bar and take two donuts from three donuts. What do you have?

Answer: Unless you have the I.Q. of a gnat, you'd know if you take two donuts from three donuts you still have three donuts! Gees! Also, while you're touching all those donuts, with your filthy hands you better buy them...

5. Two senators play Chess, each plays five games without a draw, yet each wins the same number of games. How could this ever, ever happen?

Answer: When two senators play chess or any other board game, play the same number of games and each wins the same number of games without a draw, then these two people, as any schmuck could tell, weren't playing each other. They should also have their paychecks docked for screwing off this way.

6. A Carson City doctor gave a legislator three pills for an undisclosed illness and told her to take one pill every half hour. How long would the pills last?

Answer: 'Here's three pills. Take one now and then one each half hour. The legislator will be out of pills in one hour unless she gives them to that cute lobbyist she's been eyeballing!

7. During a six months Nevada legislative session, some months have 30 days, some have 31 days. How many months have 28 days?

Answer: If you missed this one, you're dumber than I could possibly imagine. Every month I know of has 28 days! Maybe a brain transplant would help?

8. How many birthdays does the average lobbyist have?

Answer: First off, you simpleton, there is no such thing as an average lobbyist! They're all way below average. Secondly, did you try to guess the average age of lobbyist stalking the halls? I'll just bet you did! The answer is simple, maybe not for you, but trust me on this...it's simple. Lobbyists, like other slobs on the planet, have only one birthday. They may celebrate that birthday any number of times. Jack Benny, for instance only celebrated his birthday 39 times, but that wasn't the point, was it?

9. If a lobbyist goes to bed at eight tonight and sets his wind-up alarm clock for nine tomorrow morning, how much sleep does he get?

Answer: Hey, stay with me on this one, you ignoramus! A wind-up clock doesn't know if it's AM or PM, right! So he goes to bed at eight and sets it for nine. He gets one hour's sleep! That is, if he goes right to sleep and if he's alone, but don't get me started!

10. A female lobbyist contributes $500 to the election campaign of a legislator. The lobbyist is the legislator's sister, but the legislator is not the lobbyist's brother." How come?

Answer: Don't think too hard on this one, you might give your brain a hernia! The legislator is a woman. You're stereotyping again, aren't you?!

11. A lobbyist has two bills he is trying to stuff into the pocket of a legislator to assure his vote. The bills total fifty five dollars. (Cheap, huh?) One of the bills is not a fiver. What are the bills?

Answer: Two bills add up to fifty five dollars, OK? There's only one way this can happen. If you had the brains of a Peruvian cavvy, you'd have figured this one out! If one bill ain't a five dollar bill...then the other one has to be a five dollar bill, right?

12. Why can't a lobbyist living north of the Carson River be buried south of the Carson River?

Answer: When is the last time you tried to bury a lobbyist who was still alive? Maybe, if you'd call me...I'd come help you bury a live legislator or two...anytime!

The way I got it figured, you're a meshugne and you busted your lobbyists finals! Why don't you get an honest job like the rest of us schmoes and quit brown-nosing those people, who, if they didn't have a vote, you would avoid like they had syphilis! If you ever get a clue, also try to get a life!

❧

LEGISLATIVE VIGNETTES

Toward the end of each Nevada legislative session there are long periods of boredom for legislators and lobbyist. One Assemblyman in particular usually breaks out his guitar and holds sing-a-longs, others might watch TV in the lounges. The legislative shutting-down process has a mind of its own

232

and will not be rushed.

One year it was announced there would be an 'ugly tie contest' and lobbyists and legislators were directed to wear their most hideous cravats. It just so happened, a lobbyist won the contest wearing an ultra wide, stripped, paisley tie with international orange polka dots; it was a thing to behold! When the selection committee approached him with the prize, a lunch for two at Adela's restaurant in Carson City, he was oblivious of the contest...did not know there was a contest!

❦

FINE THREADS!

There is a certain stodginess among certain lobbyists when it comes to fancy clothes. The money each lobbyist makes really has no bearing on the quality or stylishness of the clothes they wear. For example, certain highly paid lobbyists buy outrageously expensive clothes, but look like hell in them because they are so grossly overweight or they never have those 'Georgio Armani' suits cleaned. Women lobbyist don't figure in on this, they are always well and tastefully dressed.

This one lobbyist was shopping at Macy's in Reno one evening just before the legislature opened and met another lobbyist he'd not seen since the previous session. One lobbyist to another:

"Clarence, this session I'm going to present a new image. I'm going to buy some tasteful suits, some stylish shirts, some with-it shoes and some killer ties. The sky's the limit...costs be damned!"

The second lobbyist had to bite his tongue to keep from

saying something catty! He said nothing. The first lobbyist continued,

"You always look so well dressed Clarence! What is it? We buy our clothes at the same places, why is it you always look so dapper? I never get any compliments, why is that?" Clarence could not pass up this once in a lifetime opportunity to give some solicited advice...catty as it might be! "Well, Philip, it's because I don't sleep in my clothes!"

❦

PRESIDENTIAL MATERIAL!

There was a joke going around about a certain member of the assembly who was quite promiscuous. He had a tag sewn into all his trousers that read "If found, please call 702-555-6356 REWARD!"

❦

PASS AND FAIL

Joe Comforte, the owner of the world famous 'Mustang Ranch' brothel on the out-skirts of Reno (pun intended) used to court the favor of Nevada legislators. He was always fearful a bill to outlaw brothels in the smaller counties might sneak through the legislature. Each session he would see to it that legislators received free 'passes' to the 'Mustang Ranch' and though there were few actual users of these 'comps' among legislators, these passes became collectors' items.

One Assemblyman, whose wife accompanied him each

session, opened his wallet and showed her his newly acquired 'pass,' she commented emphatically,

"You better always have that in your possession and never lose it!"

❦

SNAKE OIL

There was testimony on a bill in the 70's to permit the manufacture and use in Nevada of a substance that would re-create youth, vitality and vigor! The name of this elixir must remain nameless, but it was touted to be miraculously successful in some third world countries. This mess could never, ever get approved through the federal food and drug administration...not in one million years! These lobbyists would bring it to Nevada, get a slew of testimonials and overpower this little legislature like most everybody else did if they had enough clout.

There was copious testimony in support of this snake oil. The bill passed and this passage was influenced by the testimony of one senior Senator who commented in hearing, "Before I started taking this wonder drug, I had trouble hitting my drive more than 100 yards. Now I can easily hit the ball over 125 yards!"

❦

PARTING SHOT

When he retired after twenty years as a legislative advocate, this aging lobbyist was quoted as saying.

"Twenty years ago, I thought the Nevada legislature was collectively the dumbest group of misfits on the face of the planet. Today as I enter my retirement, I am convinced of it!"

NOT A UNIQUE EXPERIENCE

The Nevada legislature got a significant scare in the mid seventies. There was this ex-brothel madam/prostitute in the Hawthorn area who decided to run for the state assembly. She ran as good a campaign as the other candidate and her campaign was doing remarkably well. Election night campaign headquarters held in one of the downtown bars in Hawthorn, was full of excited supporters as the results came in election night. The election was hers at 1:00 AM, but when she awoke on Wednesday morning she had suffered an unexplainable narrow defeat. The story goes that she gathered her supporters together, thanked them, and exclaimed, "Sometime during the night, I got screwed!"

DYNAMIC DUO

Jesse Winchester, another retired madam/prostitute in Nevada has garnered substantial name recognition through out the state in recent years for offering for public office. In 1996 she ran for the U.S. House of Representatives on the Democratic ticket. Were you to hear her platform you'd think she was just another candidate, but there was something about her background that would make you feel uncomfortable with her representing you in Washington. In 1997, Ms. Winchester let it be known she was not going to be a Democrat anymore because of the way she was treated during her last campaign. The republicans did not exactly open their arms and wallets when she declared for Lt. Governor under their banner either! Some wag made the comment politicians were not that unfamiliar with prostitution and that prostitutes and politicians had a great deal in common!

Here is how a bill becomes law in Nevada:

1. Lobbyist prepares bill and gives to legislator for introduction.
2. Legislator sits on bill...ponders it.
3. Lobbyist threatens to withhold campaign contributions.
4. Legislator sends bill to friends and relatives for review.
5. Bill altered beyond all recognition then sent to the Legislative Council Bureau.
6. Bill rewritten and introduced by committee so no one can ever know who wrote this monster.
7. Bill read first time, referred to unrelated committee for hearing.
8. Bill passes first chamber then laid off on other chamber.
9. Bill goes through same process, but not as fast.
10. Governor's aides try to rewrite bill.
11. Bill re-referred to ways and means for financing.

12. Bill grossly underfunded.
13. Governor threatens veto if passed.
14. Bill passes after ignoring Governor's threats.
15. Governor signs bill into law with lobbyist present for pictures.
16. The people of Nevada reap the benefits of the bill, if any.

This has been a small collection of my favorite stories about Nevada's cities, small communities, physicians and its legislature. Nothing mean or hurtful here!

The state is becoming far too complex and its citizens far too serious. Humor may soon be in short supply because of this complexity and seriousness. There have been dramatic changes over the years and most of us who have been here some time have not liked many of them. Still we all sing the praises of our Nevada even though it might encourage others to move here! I'll continue to do what I can to inject a little levity into this inevitably changing social and political landscape.

In closing allow me to tell you about the Nevada I have loved for over a quarter century:

I LOVE THREE NEVADAS

I love Nevada...Love it!
Those spinning wheels...Happy dice!
Slot machines...Flashing lights,
Big name entertainers,
Food!...Good...Cheap and fast!
Exciting stage shows,
Wedding chapels,
Jackpot noises,
Visitors
Winning
Cash!
And
I love the mountains...Everywhere!
Snow capped, dark and foreboding.
Sagebrushes...Lots of them.
Quaking aspens...desert,
Pinions, Joshuas,
Coyotes, Jacks, Horses,
Electric Air!
An illusive
Mountain Lion
Stalking
Deer.

But
I love Nevada's Spirit!
Love it best of all! Fabric!
A counterpane...Patchwork
Composed of a million
Relocated hearts
Here for a new chance.
With hopes rising
For a better
Life. It's here!
Take off!
Soar!

End